THE SECRETS SERIES

THE SECRETS OF PRAYER

When Death Knocked at My Door
The 5 Moments that Changed My Life

A Narrative Nonfiction Work

By Lori Ann Moeszinger

Memoir

The Secrets of Prayer

When Death Knocked at My Door: The 5 Moments that Changed My Life

A Narrative Nonfiction Work

Autobiography

Total Surrender: My Story

and Your Blueprint for a Meaningful Life

Christian Living Series

Passion for Christ: New Beginnings

The Living Waters Series

Faith On Trial: The Startling Reality of Genuine Belief

Drenched in Faith: The Transformative Act of Water Baptism

Spirit Filled Life: The Unseen Force of Divine Power

The Bible Unbound: Trust, Translation, and Transformation

Prophets and Pulpits: Discerning Truth in the House of God

Beyond the Tithe: The Transformative Power of Generous Faith

Heart of Abundance: The Journey to Radical Giving and Receiving

Heaven's Reach: Drawing the Unbelieving into the Fold

Breaking Silence: The Charge to Uphold the Faith Out Loud

Beyond the Final Breath: The Christian's Voyage into Eternity

Christian Living Series

In Sacred Conversation: The New Testament Prayer Guide

THE SECRETS SERIES

THE SECRETS OF PRAYER

When Death Knocked at My Door
The 5 Moments that Changed My Life

A Narrative Nonfiction Work

By

Lori Ann Moeszinger

Urban Chronicles Publishing House
an imprint of The Ridge Publishing Group
Coeur d'Alene, Idaho, U.S.A.

Library of Congress Control Number: 2024916246

When Death Knocked at My Door: The 5 Moments that Changed My Life by Lori Ann Moeszinger

ISBN 978-1-956905-04-5 (e-book)
ISBN 978-1-956905-05-2 (soft cover)
ISBN 978-1-956905-06-9 (hard cover)

1. Biography & Autobiography—Personal Memoirs. 2. Health & Fitness—Health Care Issues. 3. Medical—Health Policy. 4. Social Science—Disease & Health Issues. 5. Medical—Gynecology & Obstetrics. I. Title.

Printed in the United States of America

NOTE TO THE READER

The information contained in this book should by no means be construed as a substitute for the advice of a qualified medical professional, who should always be consulted before self-diagnosing any health issues. This publication is intended to provide helpful and informative material. It is not intended to diagnose, treat, cure, or prevent any health problem or condition, nor is it intended to replace the advice of a physician. No action should be taken solely on the contents of this book. Always consult your physician or qualified healthcare professional on any matters regarding your health and before adopting any suggestions in this book or drawing inferences from it.

CONTENTS

ACKNOWLEDGMENTS

I am forever indebted to the medical community that worked so hard to save my life. Please note that this book is in no way sponsored by anyone in the medical community, and they reserve all rights to publish a book of their own in the future.

To the wonderful Urban Chronicles Publishing House, an imprint of The Ridge Publishing Group, who saw a cause "endometriosis" under supported and took a chance on my story.

None of this would be possible without the unconditional love and support of my parents. Thank you!

Lastly, how can I adequately thank my brilliant, handsome, and wonderful husband — the best man I ever married and the last one I'll ever need. My children are a source of joy and pride. Their support and love mean everything to me.

Finally, thank you God for answering my prayers and taking a chance on me with your Word!

THE SECRETS SERIES

THE SECRETS OF PRAYER

When Death Knocked at My Door
The 5 Moments that Changed My Life

A Narrative Nonfiction Work

Symptoms

Okay, so I was having a bad day. I'd visited the ladies room non-stop; it seemed like I needed to pee every ten minutes! I was experiencing a lot of abdominal pain and I noticed I was moving slower than usual—something was not right.

Although I had always seen my doctor on an annual basis, I was now seeing her semi-annually because of my chronic symptoms. Still my symptoms were always diagnosed the same, "pre-menopausal symptoms," but now I was having a new symptom—frequent urination with little output. So I decided to call my doctor and make an unscheduled appointment.

I had met my doctor years ago when she joined the medical group I had been going to since I was the age of seven. Preferring a female doctor, I switched to her somewhere in my early thirties. Years later, she spun off her own practice, relocating nearby where I followed her. In fact, even my prior doctor—one of the founding members of the medical group—decided to join her practice.

I arrived at my doctor's office at 9:00 a.m. and was seen shortly thereafter. During my visit, I explained to her my new symptoms and rehashed my old ones—nonetheless no progress. Still, she thought I was experiencing traditional "pre-menopausal symptoms," but this was different; this time I was scared. Intuitively, I knew something was wrong. Frustrated, I insisted my condition was getting worse and so I asked her for more testing. She listened and agreed to authorize an ultrasound, which I could schedule subsequently at a medical facility of my choosing.

Happy and relieved that something was being done, I scheduled the ultrasound for the next day. When I arrived at my appointment, I was asked to undress and change into the usual dreadful hospital gown for the exam. I'd had ultrasounds before, but this appointment was bizarre. Whereas normally the technician is "mum's the word," due to protocol; this particular technician during the procedure asked me repeatedly, "Have you had any previous surgeries?"

"No—other than natural child birth and a tubal ligation," I replied. "Why?"

Of course she would not answer me. Instead, now she stuck to protocol, ignoring each of my inquiries.

Nevertheless, in spite of what became a very alarming appointment, I dismissed it and returned to work.

By the time I arrived home from work it was late afternoon. Instantly, I noticed I had three messages on my answering machine. As I played each message I got more and more alarmed—the messages indicated that it was "urgent that I contact my doctor's office immediately." So I grabbed a pen and paper, and replayed the messages one more time, writing down what little information the caller had left.

Afterwards, I called my doctor's office and was transferred to her. My doctor told me that I needed to immediately see an obstetrician/gynecologist (OB/GYN) specialist with respect to my ultrasound findings. She referred me to a colleague, who I will call, Dr. X. She explained that the ultrasound indicated fibroids on my uterine walls and a large cyst on one of my ovaries. She explained that Dr. X would also perform his own exam in his office to confirm the ultrasound findings.

Needless to say, I was shocked and frightened with all the drama that had just transpired. I knew now that something was very wrong. I also knew something had been wrong for quite some time. Hence, my continued visits to my doctor with respect to my chronic symptoms— the same symptoms that were always diagnosed "pre-menopausal symptoms." As I pondered my new reality, I called my husband and broke down in tears.

"I just got home and there were three messages on our answering machine telling me to immediately contact my doctor's office," I sobbed.

He silently listened.

Barely catching my breath, "It's something to do with my ultrasound findings and now I have to see a specialist TODAY!"

"Calm down sweetie . . . don't worry . . . I am on my way home" he reassured me. "I love you."

"Love you too," I said.

After regaining control of myself, I called Dr. X's office and made an appointment for 4:30 p.m. that afternoon. It seemed as though they had been expecting my call. As I wrote down the directions the receptionist had given me, I was thankful his office was not far and that I was familiar with the area.

In the meantime—while playing the waiting game—I wanted to keep myself occupied. So I nervously did a Google search on Dr. X. I found that he did indeed have a website and on the surface his credentials appeared to support my doctor's recommendation; and so, I felt at ease.

A half hour later, my husband arrived home and drove me to my appointment. Upon arrival, I was served the usual clipboard and forms to fill out. While my husband and I took a seat, I couldn't help but notice how different Dr. X's office looked. His lobby reminded me more of a living room setting than a doctor's office; two couches and a loveseat with coffee table, cocktail table, and two end tables. After completing the forms I returned them to the receptionist, picked out a magazine, and nestled in close to my husband.

Next, Dr. X, who was accompanied by his nurse, saw me. He had a pleasant bedside manner, warm and friendly, not too tall, seemed fit, and wore the traditional white doctor's coat over his street clothes. In the exam room, he had his own ultrasound equipment next to the bed and off to the side was a curtained changing room.

After the customary greetings, his nurse offered me a gown and ushered me to the changing room. While I was changing the two of them prepared for my exam. Upon my return, I was then asked to lie down on the exam table while Dr. X performed his own ultrasound.

"I can see that you have fibroids on the walls of your uterus and a cyst on your left ovary," Dr. X confirmed.

"Is this why my body seems to have taken on a pregnancy position?" I asked.

"Yes—your fibroids and cyst are quite large and can be compared to a woman who is five months pregnant," he said.

"So what happens next?" I asked anxiously.

"Go ahead and get dressed . . . and if your husband is here, why don't the two of you meet me in my office down the hall," he replied, gesturing down the hallway. "We can talk about next steps there."

After getting dressed, I poked my head into the waiting room and motioned for my husband to join me. He quickly put his magazine down and eyeglasses back in his pocket as he got up to follow me. Together, we entered Dr. X's office and exchanged introductions.

"Good afternoon," Dr. X said, extending his hand to my husband.

"Good afternoon," my husband replied, shaking Dr. X's hand.

"As I've told your wife, the ultrasound results confirm she has uterine fibroids and a large cyst on one of her ovaries. There are two options. She could live with the condition and I can prescribe her something for the pain or we could perform a hysterectomy removing the fibroids and cyst along with her ovaries and uterus."

"Living in chronic pain—on pain pills—is not an option," my husband said, shaking his head.

I whole-heartedly agreed with him; so with a nod and a smile I gave my agreement.

"I concur," Dr. X said. "The fibroids have completely taken over the right ovary and the left one doesn't appear to have fared any better—deteriorating to almost nothing. Consequently, I recommend a complete hysterectomy as opposed to a partial."

Being in our forties, my husband and I were not interested in having children of our own; therefore, a hysterectomy was not an issue for us. Especially if it meant that the fibroids and cyst that were causing me so much pain and fatigue would be gone.

"I agree. I would like to opt for a complete hysterectomy," I said.

"Okay," Dr. X said. "I'll write an order for a blood test so that we can rule out cancer. I will be your only surgeon unless you test positive for cancer, in which case I will be accompanied by a surgeon specializing in oncology."

Next, he wrote me a prescription for Vicodin to ease the pain. My husband and I then thanked him and together the three of us walked to his nurses' station. There, he handed me "doctor's orders" for my blood work and directed us to a lab around the corner within the same office complex. He then shuffled through his schedule selecting a date for my surgery; nearly four weeks away, that seemed a long ways off to me but I didn't object.

After that, my husband and I were off to find the lab. As usual, I thought we should go in one direction and he thought we should go in another. Nonetheless, as I was in no condition to argue I gave in and followed. He was right and we found the lab.

Again I would be given a clipboard with forms to fill out before I could be seen. Surprisingly, I was called right away following my registration. After my blood had been drawn I rejoined my husband and together we walked to our vehicle.

Although not feeling well and still in pain, I was relieved that something was being done. I was also armed with a prescription for Vicodin—a feel good drug I had heard so much about, but was hesitant to try. However, since surgery wasn't imminent, I was glad to have something to ease my pain while I waited the nearly four weeks until surgery.

I chalked all this drama up to my "parts" getting older and hysterectomies a routine remedy for "parts gone bad." I believed I was in good hands. After all, my doctor, who I'd been seeing for years, recommended Dr. X. I'd even done a Google search and he had checked out fine.

Feeling relieved and wanting to decompress, I decided to talk my husband into taking me to dinner. This would not be hard to do nor would it be new to my husband. With both of us working in demanding professions in law and technology—coupled with the fact that I didn't cook unless we were entertaining—we went out to eat a lot.

"Honey—do you mind if we go downtown tonight and have dinner at Tarragon?" I cooed.

This was one of our favorite hot spots.

"After dinner we can hit one of the local bars nearby to relax."

My husband had been a confirmed bachelor until the age of forty when he met the woman of his dreams—me! Until he met me, it was always work followed by the local sports bar scene with his friends. I mean this was a ritual, six, seven days a week. On top of that—like many men—he was scared to death of the "M" word! But all that changed after he met me. Now his friends tell him, "marrying" me probably added twenty years to his life.

"Great sweetie—that sounds good," he replied excitedly.

"Should we call for a cab, since God knows I can't walk?"

Downtown was less than a mile away from our apartment. Before my condition, we often walked to our favorite dining places, followed by cocktails at local hot spots. Afterwards we always took a cab home—paying for just a one-way fare, but now we would be paying for a round trip fare.

"Sounds good," he replied. "I will call a cab after we fill your prescription and return home."

"Thank you, honey."

No, I was not supposed to be drinking while taking Vicodin—nor had I ever taken Vicodin before for that matter. Yet, in spite of everything, I felt I had just dodged a bullet and believed everything would be fine following my upcoming surgery. Things were looking up. I'd have time off from work, no more cramps or menstrual periods, no more pain—or so I thought . . .

Affairs in Order

In the meantime, between my initial visit with Dr. X and the date of my upcoming hysterectomy, I would continue on with my life—but it would not be life as I had known. I was quickly deteriorating. Vicodin was not working and I really didn't like taking pills in the first place. As a wife, mother, employee, and serial entrepreneur, I thrived on being productive and it required a clear head. So I was really looking forward to getting my life back on track following my surgery.

Upcoming Company Launch

As a forty-seven year old woman, I had taken the traditional route. My priorities were marriage, children, education, and then entrepreneurship. Married with children and degrees in business and law, I was now working towards my dream of building a fashion and luxury goods business. Eighteen months prior, I had started laying the foundation for this significant "up and coming" company. With twenty-plus years of experience in corporate law, mergers and acquisitions, public offerings, fundraisings, and spin-offs, the time had come for me to become chief executive officer (CEO) of my own company.

In addition to my many years of practical experience in business and the arts, I had spent years studying the success of two men I consider my role models, Warren Buffet and Donald Trump. Whereas Mr. Buffet's story taught me patience, loyalty, and kindness—much like him, I don't take risks unless I have done my homework. Mr. Trump's story, on the other hand, has taught me the difference between planners and implementers. While a planner is always planning and never implements, an implementer executes his or her plans. Drawing upon these lessons, coupled with more than twenty years of experience working alongside CEOs, I was well prepared to launch my company following my hysterectomy and recovery period.

My plan was to start with fundraising activities. In addition to a teaser presentation in the form of a three-page invitation, I was armed with a formal presentation, supporting business plan, confidentiality and non-disclosure agreements, and term sheets. As well, I had a list of target investors to solicit and ultimately obtain funding from.

With my surgery out of the way and my health in order, my timing could not have been more perfect. It was 2007, the economy was booming and investors were "chomping at the bit" for new places to invest their money. Not to mention, housing was at an all time high, unemployment was under four percent, and the stock market was reaching new highs every day—it seemed I couldn't lose. I was jazzed and excited to get this train rolling towards a new phase of my life creating my own legacy.

But first and foremost, I needed my health in order. I knew any potential investors would not be interested in such an investment, if the "key man or woman" was having health issues. Although I am sure that there are many men out there who would disagree with me and choose to move forward regardless. My integrity, however, would not allow me to do so until after my surgery and ultimate recovery. Furthermore, I would not have confidence in any investor who was not thorough enough in their due diligence to discover such a potentially serious issue.

Employer

I kept working for my employer until two days before my hysterectomy was scheduled. My position had been newly created within the company, to give in-house legal a local presence. My boss, the general counsel, primarily represented the company from out of state. With little to do most days, I had the luxury of working on my own endeavors as long as I was onsite in case someone locally needed legal services.

Most recently, I had been reviewing and editing my website content, which had been previously designed and uploaded in preparation for the launch of my fashion house. In addition, I had recently completed the initial application process for a garment manufacturing industry certificate of registration. I would need such a certificate before I would be able to hire employees. Hence, I was also developing the human resources intranet content for my company.

Currently, I was wrapping things up, briefing my employer as to where I would be leaving things when I left on medical leave. I had completed the state and supplemental disability paperwork with human resources early on. Finally, I packed up my personal belongings, since during my absence my employer would be moving to a new location.

Family and Home

Usually an immaculate housekeeper; my home was my sanctuary. However, with my continued deterioration, I was no longer attending to our home like I was accustomed to. In fact, I was barely able to find the energy to get to and from work. This frustrated me and made me even more miserable, but there was nothing I could do about it—I was too tired to do much of anything.

Where it had always been routine for my husband and I to walk to either downtown for dinner or to a local sports bar where we could eat and hang out with friends. Now, the only walking I could do was to the local areas downstairs. Living in a luxury apartment complex, we were surrounded by delis, restaurants, retail, and commercial establishments. Walking was very much a "lifestyle thing" for us.

Now, we had to make a decision about a cruise we had previously scheduled and made a deposit on. We had been going on cruises annually for several years with his parents. Our next destination was a seventeen-day cruise through the Panama Canal. After a short discussion, we decided we would take the cruise since it would follow my surgery by roughly seven months. Thus, we made the final payment as I was positive I would be fine and back to normal by then.

Premonition or Real

A couple of months before my hysterectomy, I had an eerie dream involving my grandfather—he had died nearly two and half years earlier. I was very close to my grandfather as I am close with all my family. So close that throughout my childhood, every Sunday, mom would cook a homemade meal and my grandparents (her parents) were always invited—this was a family tradition.

Moreover, during my late teens—when I was just starting out on my own—I lived on my grandparent's property in their guesthouse. In fact, I was living with them when I purchased my first car, a Cougar, which I would never drive; I was afraid of it. I thought it was too big and I couldn't figure out how—if I ever drove it—I would ever be able to keep it between the lanes on the road. So we sold it and my grandfather bought me a small Opal GT—a much smaller vehicle—in which he and my dad taught me how to drive.

In my dream, I was standing in the entryway of my parent's house looking out at the front porch. My grandfather was standing a short distance away—holding out his hand—motioning for me to come with him. He was not alone; dozens of people were with him—relatives and strangers so I thought—gathering around behind him where the crowd disappeared into the foggy distance. I didn't pay close attention or recognize any of their faces as I was focused on my grandfather and stunned by his gesture. Frightened, I screamed, "No" and abruptly woke up. I was scared.

Was this a premonition or real? Was I going to die and join my grandfather? Or was it something else? Was it not my grandfather with shoulder-length hair in the distance? Or could it have been Jesus Himself and not my grandfather at all? Were the people behind Him disciples or sinners ready for their next destination? The thoughts haunted me. It felt so real and unnerving.

For days I had kept the dream to myself, until one evening when my husband and I were at my parents' house for dinner. They could see I was miserable and preoccupied, frequently drifting off in thought. I was

13

thinking about the dream—and my grandfather's or Jesus' gesture—it was preoccupying me. So I decided to tell my parents and husband about the dream. Afterwards, they were as spooked as I had been so we changed the subject to lighter topics.

State of Mind

Throughout the time, between my initial visit to Dr. X's office and the actual surgery date, my symptoms continued to decline. Each day I had less and less energy—my normal upbeat positive self was no longer. I felt like I was running on empty and withering away. So I called Dr. X's office and asked if an earlier surgery date could be arranged. Still, in spite of how I was feeling, he did not think there was any need to move up the date.

First Brush with Death

3

It was a beautiful summer day and I was ready—the day for my surgery had finally come. My affairs were in order and I had checked in with hospital administration the day before. Even though merely a "routine hysterectomy" my parents had insisted upon accompanying my husband and me to the hospital. (They're very protective as I am their only daughter; I have three brothers.)

During preparation, my nurse was babbling on and on about how her hysterectomy was the best thing that had ever happened to her. Nonetheless, I was jazzed and excited to finally be getting things over with. It was time, family hugs and kisses were exchanged, and I was wheeled into the Operating Room. There I followed my anesthesiologist's orders to count backwards—lights out!

The surgery went too long—way too long—something was wrong. Dr. X had made a horizontal incision—nine inches long—at my bikini line to perform the hysterectomy. Surgery was only supposed to last an hour and a half but now it was nearly five hours later. No one had been out to inform my husband and parents what had happened or why it was taking so long—they were rightfully very worried. Finally, Dr. X walked into the waiting area.

"Well—I think I stopped the bleeding," Dr. X sighed.

My husband and parents were confused and troubled. Dr. X did not seem well composed and he looked exhausted. It was apparent that Dr. X was under the impression my family had already been informed and he was merely providing follow-up.

"Hold on—wait a minute. Start from the beginning, we haven't been told anything," my husband interrupted.

Dr. X, realizing his blunder, began to explain from the beginning.

"There were complications and some blood loss—but I think I stopped all the bleeding and don't think she will need to be given any blood transfusions. I really don't want to unless it's absolutely necessary."

"What complications?" my mother asked.

"As soon as I opened her up, I discovered endometriosis—it—it— it was everywhere," he said. "The worst case I have ever seen. It was all throughout her."

"Endometriosis?" my husband asked.

"Yes," Dr. X replied. "The hysterectomy was complicated by the endometriosis; there was so much of it that it had eaten away at the surrounding tissue weakening it to the point where it would not even hold a suture."

My husband and parents were silent—the news was shocking and unexpected.

Dr. X continued, "With the amount of endometriosis she had—in most cases—it would have likely gone into her bloodstream and transported to other areas of her body through the blood or lymphatic systems and killed her. Had she not had this surgery . . . in six months . . . I don't know what would have happened . . . she'd probably be dead.

"Where is she?" my mother asked trembling while holding back tears. "Can we see her?"

"She is still in Post-Op but should be moved to an inpatient room within the hour," Dr. X reassured. "You can see her then."

"So—that will be around 5:30 p.m.?" my husband asked.

"Yes! And now I need to get back to my office. I have patients waiting for me," Dr. X said abruptly.

What? Are you kidding me? If I was in such bad shape, why did Dr. X wait nearly four weeks before doing the surgery? Why wasn't the endometriosis diagnosed beforehand when he was screening for cancer? What is endometriosis? And why are you leaving? You only "think you have stopped my bleeding." What if you haven't?

Later, my mother would tell me that Dr. X's last comment really bothered her. She couldn't figure out why he would have patients waiting for him at his office when it was nearly 5:00 p.m. She instinctively felt he should have stayed with me until I was moved to an inpatient room.

Months later, I would request copies of my medical records and I would learn from the Operating Report therein that Dr. X did have a second doctor assisting him during my surgery. More questions. Who was this second doctor? Dr. X had assured me he would be the only doctor performing my surgery once cancer was ruled out. Why was Dr. X assisted? Was the second doctor an intern or an assistant?

Day 1 - Thursday

A quick recap. My hysterectomy was at 12:00 noon. Dr. X left to go back to his office to assist other patients at around 4:45 p.m. after "thinking he'd stopped my bleeding." I was still in Post-Op, and according to Dr. X, soon to be moved to an inpatient room where I could receive visitors. My husband and parents still had not seen me since I'd gone to surgery nearly five hours ago.

Once again my husband and parents—now joined by my oldest son—found themselves anxious. Several more hours had passed since Dr. X had led them to believe I would be moved to an inpatient room. Although they had been continually asking hospital staff for information, no one seemed to know anything. My family was still not sure where I was or why the hospital staff didn't have any answers.

As they waited, they had watched staff come and go—on and off shift—yet no one was approaching them. Finally, at around 7:00 p.m., my husband and parents had, had enough—they were restless and very worried. Consequently they went back up to the hospital reception desk and demanded information; this time getting answers.

They were informed that I had not been moved to an inpatient room. Instead, I had been moved from Post-Op into the hospital's Critical Care Unit (CCU) due to complications. Again, my husband and parents could not believe what they were hearing—but at least they were finally getting information.

Next, they were directed to a small waiting area just outside the CCU doors. There was a telephone on the wall in which they were instructed to pick up and inquire as to my status. Shortly thereafter a nurse came out to allow my husband into the CCU to see me for the first time. He was only inside for seconds when tears began to swell in his eyes—he couldn't believe what he was seeing.

"You were white as a ghost," he told me later. "I thought I was looking at your dead body—it was the scariest moment of my life. I never thought there was a possibility of losing you. I always just assumed I would be the one to go first."

Seconds later my anesthesiologist, who I will call, Dr. Miracle also appeared in the CCU. He had just learned "through the grapevine" that I was in the CCU. Wondering why, he dropped by to investigate. My husband, who had met Dr. Miracle earlier that morning during check-in, immediately welcomed the friendly face.

Dr. Miracle, like my husband, was visibly shocked at the sight of me. Alarmed by my vital signs—low pulse, blood pressure 80/20; even my husband knew that was bad. He quickly began issuing orders.

Obviously, I was bleeding internally and based on these numbers, close to death. Yet, no one was doing anything about it. Where were the doctors? What was the CCU staff doing? And why wasn't any blood ordered?

My blood pressure reading 80/20 indicated not only internal bleeding, but that I was in shock and dying. More alarming was the fact that the CCU staff was right there; watching me bleed to death. No one had even made any attempt to call Dr. X or order any blood. Undoubtedly, but for Dr. Miracle's curiosity, arrival, and quick reaction, I would have died in the CCU—this would be my first brush with death but unfortunately, not my last![1]

My husband was further shocked when he saw how stunned Dr. Miracle was. In my current state with the incline position the CCU staff had my bed in; he told my husband that such an incline could potentially cause my internal organs to shift into my chest cavity further complicating my condition. Clearly alarmed, he immediately began shouting orders at the surprised CCU staff.

"Reposition the bed—only the legs should be inclined to help sustain her blood pressure!" He yelled frantically. "Call for a gurney and get her scheduled for surgery immediately! Has her doctor been called? Someone get him on the phone stat—he should be here!"

My husband watched in disbelief.

"Send for blood!" Dr. Miracle snapped. "She'll need at least three units immediately."

"We sent for one unit," a nursed replied.

"Not good enough—at least three I said!" Dr. Miracle shouted back.

"Okay," the nurse replied, running out the back door to retrieve the blood.

My parents and oldest son—still sitting in the waiting room outside the CCU—watched as the nurse hurriedly ran out sprinting up the hall.

Within the frantic chaos, my husband—still in distress—realized he was only getting in the way, so he decided to leave the CCU and rejoin my parents and son. Still stunned by what he had just witnessed, he was at a loss for words. While he slowly approached my parents and son, the sight of their questioning faces only made it harder for him to speak. Tears began to well up into his eyes as he looked to the floor and tried to force the lump from his throat. Gradually he was able to regain enough composure to utter a few words.

"She's—not good!" my husband managed.

Seeing the look on his face said it all, so my parents did not press him. After a few moments he was able to say more.

"She is bleeding internally and they are giving her blood—she is going to need another surgery."

Then he sat motionless and quiet. Together, they again began to wait—not knowing what was coming next. Mom was praying, while my husband, son, and dad were deep in their own thoughts.

Moments later, they were again startled as the nurse dashed back down the hallway gripping two units of blood—she hurried straight through the CCU doors. As the doors hung open they could faintly hear Dr. Miracle's orders as the nurse entered the room.

"Get the first unit hooked up and begin administering it—stat!" Dr. Miracle said in a commanding tone. "She needs to be stabilized before we take her back to surgery!"

"Yes doctor," the nurse complied.

"We're going to need more blood than this!" Dr. Miracle ordered as the doors closed and the voices muffled away.

I was receiving my second unit of blood when Dr. X had returned to the hospital. Dr. Miracle quickly briefed him on what had occurred during his absence.

Finally, a nurse emerged from the CCU to speak with my husband. "You will need to sign this consent form right away, so we can perform an emergency surgery," she said.

My husband silently complied. He was speechless and overcome by emotion.

Then—as swiftly as was possible—I was in motion. Bursting through the CCU doors, Dr. X was at the head of my gurney pushing and running along with the orderlies. Racing me up the hall, they guided me into the elevator and back into the Operating Room.

My family would tell me later that at least seven people were assisting. But what would stay in their minds forever was the image of my surgeon, Dr. X, joining in the rush pushing me down the hallway to surgery. It would be one of the most frightening sights of their lives.

By the time my second operation was over I had been given twelve units of blood! Shockingly, the adult human body contains approximately ten to twelve units of blood—equivalent to ten to twelve pints—depending on the person's size, which makes up seven to eight percent of body weight. This was truly a close brush with death!

Are there risks associated with blood transfusions? Whose blood is inside me now? Does it matter? Later, I would research risks associated with "blood transfusions" in which I have provided my findings herein.[2]

After reading these findings, clearly Dr. X's concern, when he explained to my husband and parents that he did not want to give me blood unless it was absolutely necessary, made sense. However, in my case, the blood transfusions saved my life. So apart from any risks, they were necessary.

Thank you, Dr. Miracle, for saving my life!

Welcome to My Nightmare

Dr. X, responding to Dr. Miracle's summons, had promptly returned to the hospital. He would need to open me up again—performing a second surgery—in another attempt to stop my internal bleeding. However, before he could begin the second surgery, they needed to continue administering blood into my system to get my vital signs stabilized enough for another surgery.

Once I was stabilized they began prepping me for surgery. Then, before surgery could even begin, I stopped breathing (cardiac arrest)—my second brush with death! Later, I would read the Diagnostic Imaging Record, which indicated, "breathing stopped may have been caused by central line placement."[3/4/5]

After I was successfully resuscitated, Dr. X began my second surgery. He re-opened me elongating the original incision—from nine inches to twelve inches long—once more, at my bikini line. Again, he began suturing me internally in an effort to stop the bleeding. However, the endometriosis had so severely eaten away at my insides the weakened tissue would not hold a suture. He didn't know what else to do—he was running out of options—he needed help.

Frantically, he called for help. He called a doctor, who I will call, Dr. Lifesaver—a cancer reconstructive surgeon. Miraculously, Dr. Lifesaver was in traffic on a nearby freeway a few minutes from the hospital when he received Dr. X's frantic call. He agreed to come to the hospital to assist. However, immediately upon his arrival Dr. X turned the surgery over to Dr. Lifesaver.

Later, I would be informed, by both Drs. X and Lifesaver that an OB/GYN surgeon does not operate above the uterus but a cancer reconstructive surgeon can. Thus, Dr. Lifesaver made a new incision vertically up my abdomen—ten inches long—to open me up even more. It ran from the center of my first incision to a few inches below the center of my chest. Together, they form an upside down "T" that will forever scar my midsection.

After Dr. Lifesaver made his incision, he was astonished at how "sliced up" I was and all my multiple bleeding sites. He found sutures everywhere, including some adjacent to my ureters. (Ureters are the muscular tubes that propel urine from the kidneys to the urinary bladder connecting each kidney to the bladder.) As a consequence, it was very difficult for him to try and stop my bleeding.

As Dr. Lifesaver worked to stop the bleeding, it happened again, I stopped breathing—my third brush with death! Once again I was resuscitated, but this time I was not able to breathe on my own. As a result, they inserted a breathing tube down my throat—this would stay there throughout Post-Op and beyond—until I was able to breathe on my own once again.[6/7]

After I was resuscitated a second time, Dr. Lifesaver continued his efforts to stop my bleeding. In doing so, he discovered even more damage caused by the endometriosis; it had moved on to another organ outside my female reproductive organs. It had metastasized (transfer of disease from one organ or part of the body to another not directly connected with it) onto my bladder leaving scar tissue behind. Hence, my frequent urination symptoms.

As he removed the scar tissue from my bladder, he also found that one of my ureters had been trapped by sutures and only one of my ureters remained opened. In order for him to repair my ureter it necessitated a neocystostomy procedure (surgical procedure in which the ureter tubes are detached and re-implanted into the urinary bladder to permit drainage).

Next, he inserted a ureteral stent (a thin flexible tube threaded into the ureter to help urine drain from the kidneys to the bladder) into my ureter to reinforce the repair. He then proceeded to make two small incisions—each a half inch long—one on each side of my abdomen. To these he attached temporary external drainage bags, called JP drains, used to create suction and draw out any excess fluid from the abdominal cavity. Finally, he was able to stop my bleeding and I was stapled closed.[8]

How could this be possible? Doctors claim endometriosis is confined to the female reproductive organs. However, in my case, left undiagnosed way too long, the endometriosis had clearly moved outside of my uterus and on to my bladder where it caused extensive damage.

In addition, doctors further state that endometriosis is non-cancerous and can't kill you. Although if left undiagnosed—as in my case—endometriosis can and will eat away at other internal organs outside of the female reproductive organs. So, if endometriosis eats away enough of the internal organ(s) of its choosing, it could cause organ failure and death albeit endometriosis the indirect cause.

Even more alarming, estrogen is what feeds endometriosis. So why do doctors prescribe estrogen following a hysterectomy or menopause? We naturally get estrogen from our fat even after a hysterectomy or menopause. Since there is no cure for endometriosis, it is likely that once diagnosed, continuing on estrogen will feed the disease enabling it to survive in a woman's body. Later, I would research "endometriosis" in which I have since provided my findings herein at the end of this book—chapter 34.

Day 2 - Friday

The second surgery had lasted more than four hours and was not finished until after 3:00 a.m. the next morning. At around 4:00 a.m. Dr. X introduced Dr. Lifesaver to my husband, parents, and oldest son whom were still in the CCU waiting area. Together they explained the surgical procedures performed as well as their prognosis.

"She's been through a lot," Dr. Lifesaver said cautiously. "The internal bleeding was very bad . . . so we had to give her a lot of blood."

"My son-in-law said you had to give her several units?" my mother questioned.

"Actually—she's been given twelve units," he answered.

"That's a lot of blood," my mother said. "How do we know how safe the blood is?"

"I can assure you, our blood supply is triple-checked, and there is no need to worry about the quality of the blood," Dr. X quickly interjected.

"I had to make another incision to open her up wider to see where all the bleeding was coming from," Dr. Lifesaver continued, pausing for a second. "When I did so I saw that her bladder and one of her ureters were in bad shape. Her bladder was full of scar tissue from the endometriosis. So I went ahead and repaired the damage and was able to stop her bleeding as well."

"Is she going to be okay?" my husband asked.

"She has stabilized and is in Post-Op at the moment," Dr. Lifesaver reassured. "But like I said—her ureter and bladder were in very bad shape. So I had to perform a neocystostomy—a surgical procedure in which I detached the ureter and re-implanted it back into the bladder at a site with healthier tissue. As part of the procedure, I also implanted a ureteral stent into the damaged ureter that will reinforce it and help to keep it open. She also has two external drainage devices in place— JP drains—commonly used after abdominal surgeries to help pull excess fluids from the body."

"When can we see her?" my dad asked anxiously.

"I wouldn't expect her out of Post-Op any sooner than 9:00 a.m.," Dr. Lifesaver answered. "She will be moved back into the CCU. However, there is one more thing I need to tell you."

The life was now slowly draining out of my husband, parents, and son. They had, had no sleep and they too were suffering. Nobody was prepared for what we were all going through.

27

"For now she has a breathing tube down her throat to assist her breathing—she stopped breathing during surgery," Dr. Lifesaver explained, treading as lightly as he could.

My husband, parents, and son were speechless.

"It's late now and everyone is tired," Dr. Lifesaver said. "She is doing better now—so go ahead and go home to get some sleep. You should all be able to see her in the morning."

"Thank you, thank you so much," my husband said extending his hand to both doctors; shaking hands first with Dr. Lifesaver and then with Dr. X.

"Dr. Lifesaver deserves all the thanks . . . he saved her life," Dr. X admitted. "I was at my wits end . . . I didn't know what else to do."

"It was a joint effort—we both did our part," Dr. Lifesaver humbly added.

"Thank you doctors," my dad said.

"Thank you and God bless you both," mom said.

"Thanks," my son said extending his hand to both doctors.

My husband, parents, and son retreated to my parents' house. They were overwhelmed and distraught. They had no idea what my outcome would be; I was still touch and go. This would be the first of many nights that they would gather to try to make sense of things.

I awoke with a violent jolt. I had been moved from Post-Op back into the CCU and was conscious for the first time since the first surgery. Where was I? What had happened to me? And what was this thing down my throat gagging me?

Seemingly seconds later, I remembered seeing my husband and my mom peering down at me. It was strange—I was like a wild animal that even I did not recognize. My arms were strapped down and I was angry with my husband. I kept trying to motion to him—pleading with him—to remove the breathing tube from my throat. But when he wouldn't I grew angry with him. Although I could see myself acting out I did not know why. It was not me; it was almost like an out of body experience.

My husband told me later, "Your mom seemed to have a calming effect on you, but with me it was exactly the opposite; my presence seemed to agitate you. So we all agreed that I should stay away until you were in a more stable condition."

Later, I would learn that the doctors had put me on a drug called "Ativan" in which I have since researched herein—which had caused my adverse reaction.[9]

For the rest of the day, I was in and out of consciousness. I had been assigned a wonderful nurse, who I will call, nurse-Godsend. She had a Swedish accent and was very caring, immediately winning my trust. She explained that there was residual vaginal bleeding—a normal occurrence after a hysterectomy—so she had packed me with pads and would continue to do so until it stopped.

Later that morning I met yet another doctor, whom I will call, Dr. Y. After formal introductions, he and nurse-Godsend removed my breathing tube; substituting it with oxygen that would be administered through my nose. I had finally stabilized.

Dr. Y was a very interesting doctor. It seemed as though he had done his homework with respect to my history and background. Shortly after introducing himself, he mentioned that he was attending law school—just as I had—and coincidently at the same law school. He also volunteered that he and my husband had been talking which is why he had knowledge of my background.

Nevertheless, I would never forget his parting words. He told me that he was the head of the CCU for the hospital in addition to being a practicing doctor there. He told me he had observed both of my surgeries and that it would behoove me—after discharge—to review my records so that I would know exactly what had happened during my surgeries. After which, he warned me about post-traumatic stress disorder (PTSD). At the time, I thought his whole conversation was creepy.

Hot Blooded

My God! I felt like I was on fire. Sweat was pouring out of me. I had long hair and I was miserable. Apparently, after a hysterectomy, immediately one goes directly into menopause and what I was experiencing was the usual "hot flashes." This was something I was not prepared for. No one had explained this dynamic, nor did it ever occur to me that of course a hysterectomy would throw me directly into the frying pan—okay, I mean menopause, but you get the picture.

"Nurse-Godsend," I pleaded. "I am dying over here. I feel like I am on fire! Could you please help me get my hair off my neck?"

"Yes—yes," she replied.

"Is my overnight bag here?" I asked.

"Yes—directly behind your head on a table," she answered.

"There should be a hair tie and brush in the front zipper pocket," I instructed.

I was amazed that I was cognizant enough to remember that the first pocket in my overnight bag had a hair tie and brush in it. This was good news. I felt like I was going to be whole again.

"Here they are—I found both," she said. "Can you tilt your head down for me?"

As she was brushing my hair I could feel the knots. I could tell the brush was barely making any progress at all. As she pulled and tugged away, she tried her best to be as gentle as possible. Then she abruptly stopped.

"I am not sure what to do here," she said. "There is a large chunk of hair at the nape of your neck that seems to be coated in dried blood. I can't break it up with the brush."

"If you have scissors—please just cut it off," I whined.

At that point I didn't care if I had to cut it all off. I couldn't bare it anymore. I was miserable.

"Okay—give me a second," she said.

And, relief! Bye-bye twelve-inch long chunk of hair, I remembered thinking. With that act, somehow my hot flashes seemed more manageable now that my hair was on top of my head and not laying on my neck.

At around 4:00 p.m. nurse-Godsend informed me she would soon be going off shift. It was Friday night and she told me that another nurse would be managing my care throughout the weekend.

He had arrived, and over the next hour, I listened as nurse-Godsend trained this male nurse who was supposed to take over my care. Alarmingly, she was training him on simple things such as, how to take my blood pressure, how to check my vitals, and how to document the results. I was shocked—shouldn't he already know all that? I was in the CCU in a very fragile state and it seemed someone with little to no experience was going to take over my care.

"Nurse-Godsend," I called out sweetly wanting to get her attention before she went off shift.

"Yes?" she answered.

"Is a trainee going to be taking over my care?" I inquired ever so quietly.

"Nooo—he's not a trainee," she assured me. "Since the hospital doesn't schedule surgeries on weekends, typically, the CCU is staffed with personnel from a temporary agency. I am just explaining to him how we do things here."

"Okay—it was just making me a little nervous listening to you explain to him things I assumed he should already know."

"Being a privately-held hospital, this allows our regular staff to work Monday through Friday, which is unheard of in larger hospitals," she continued. "It also serves as one of our recruitment tools—the perks of working here as opposed to the alternative larger hospitals."

Still, this was shocking to me, as I was still in a critical condition. I was full of staples. I still had a catheter connected to me that would require periodic draining. My lower legs were strapped to sequential compression devices that would periodically massage them helping to prevent blood clots. My pads would need to be changed and repacked—ongoing—since I was still bleeding vaginally. My bandages would need to be changed and incisions cleaned and redressed at least twice a day. And the drainage bags hanging off the sides of my midsection would need to be periodically drained. I looked like the bride of Frankenstein!

How in the world was this new nurse going to care for me if he was not familiar with the hospital's procedures? This was not acceptable—I thought. Nevertheless, nurse-Godsend clocked out and left for the weekend. Shortly thereafter, I decided to have a conversation with my new nurse.

"Excuse me?" I called.

"Yes," he answered, seemingly surprised.

"Can I ask you a question?"

"Yes."

"Are you a registered nurse?" I asked, thinking it would be less rude if I asked him if he was "registered" as opposed to "are you really a nurse?"

"Well—I am a nurse—but not from the United States," he answered.

"Ohhh—so have you worked for other hospitals in the U.S. before?" I asked.

"No—this is my first job in the U.S. as a nurse," he answered. "So I am not real familiar with local procedures."

I sat in silence feeling dumfounded and defeated.

"But I assure you—I am a nurse," he said.

Unbelievable! I demanded to see a doctor—but no doctor would arrive. Of course not. It was Friday night and apparently they had all clocked out for the weekend.

Frustrated, I got vocal about my displeasure in my newly appointed nurse. Subsequently, I was reassigned to an experienced nurse from the inpatient ward. She too was very nice and took an immediate liking to me or at least seemed to like being in the CCU instead of the inpatient ward she had previously been assigned.

She was very helpful in keeping cold compresses on my forehead, trying to manage my hot flashes. Mercifully, I still had an epidural in place to help with my pain management. Routinely, she would take my blood pressure every hour and then my temperature every so often. Lab technicians were in and out to draw my blood. She drained my catheter bag, drained my abdomen bags, and so on.

After several hours of this—non-stop poking and probing—I was getting irritable. I knew to recover I needed to sleep, but sleeping was impossible under the circumstances. So I snapped a bit, expressing my frustration, and she backed off. Finally, I fell asleep. Not sure if it was because the nurse backed off or out of my pure exhaustion—probably both.

Day 3- Saturday

It was day three and I was still in the CCU with yet another nurse. I was conscious more than not now. I still had the epidural in my back, so I was not aware of any pain associated with my mid-section. However, early that morning, I noticed that I was experiencing severe pain in my left leg.

I asked that the compression devices be removed from my lower legs, but the hospital staff refused. They explained that they were under "doctor's orders" that they stay on my legs. Their purpose was to increase the circulation in my legs and help prevent blood clots. So I asked to speak to a doctor, but was told that the on-call doctor would not be on rounds until early evening. Later I would research "sequential compression devices" and provide my findings herein.[10]

Moments later, my mom arrived. As we were visiting, two physical therapists showed up to work with me. They told me they were under "doctor's orders" to get me up and moving my muscles. They were both fully dressed in scrubs and had a walker with them. Unbelievable—I thought.

Are you kidding me? I just went through two major surgeries in the last seventy-two hours. I was very weak and I had very little nourishment in me. I was full of staples and my incisions were beginning to ooze. For all I knew, if I tried to stand up, my guts might drop out. Okay, so I was exaggerating, but this was how I felt—and yes, I had bandages covering my incisions holding me together.

Finally, my lower legs were freed—the nurse had taken the sequential compression devices off—albeit only temporarily so I could undergo my physical therapy. Mysteriously, even without the devices, I was still experiencing severe pain in my left leg; taking them off did not help. Once again, I was scared and nervous—more alarms were sounding off in my head.

As my mom sat watching, I warned the physical therapists that my left leg was still hurting me and both of my legs felt very weak—but they ignored my pleas. Instead, they approached me, one on either side, and helped move me into a sitting position for the first time in days. I made it! I thought—and my guts were not falling out.

Then it happened. I had warned them. They tried to stand me up and I almost fell to the floor. Immediately, they agreed that I was too weak for the physical therapy exercises they had planned. Subsequently, I was placed back in bed and the annoying devices were re-strapped to my lower legs.

It was Saturday evening and still no doctor had come to check on me. I guess nurse-Godsend was right when she said, "we have very little staff over the weekends." Oddly, hot flashes seemed to have gotten a bit better. I was not sure if they had given me any medication for them or what. Moreover, it seemed to be eerily quiet in the CCU.

My husband and parents had been circulating—in and out—visiting me as often as they could while I was in the CCU. My husband, a white collar professional in the technology sector, had complete support from his boss and was able to spend as much time with me as he needed. My father was retired and spent the mornings with me. My mother was soon to be retired and it became routine, after a quick dinner, for her and dad to return to the hospital and stay with me until my husband was off work. I was a pretty lucky girl to have all this support.

Do I have kids? Yes—three boys from a couple of different husbands. My husband now, who is the love of my life, I call my "third victim." He says he doesn't mind since he knows my ex-husbands are still alive. He has no kids of his own and this is his first marriage. He met my younger to boys when they were four and nine years old. My oldest son was living out of state at the time.

My oldest son is grown now and on his own. As for my other two sons, they were still in school and lived with their dad. My husband and I have the boys every other weekend and then some. At the time of my surgeries, they were out of state on vacation with their dad. I didn't want to interrupt their vacation, so they had not yet been told what was happening to me.

War-huh

It was Saturday evening and I knew no doctors would be around. Tonight my husband would be picking up a friend from the airport and would miss the CCU visiting hours. I was bored out of my mind and wanted to see my hubby. I rationalized that no one at the hospital was paying any attention to me. I hadn't been bathed. I hadn't even been offered a toothbrush for that matter. So I talked my husband into coming by later that evening—post-visiting hours.

It was around 8:00 p.m. when he finally arrived—he had made it! No one even questioned him, but he would only stay about a half hour; we didn't want them to think we were taking advantage of the situation. During our visit, my husband mentioned that my employer had sent a get-well bouquet of fruit to our apartment. I had totally forgotten that my employer had no idea that I was still in the hospital. So I asked my husband to call my boss the next morning and update him on my status. Shortly thereafter we said our goodnights—kiss-kiss—then my husband was gone.

Day 4- Sunday

Day four and yet another nurse from the temporary agency was assigned to me. Correction, she was not even a nurse. She was either a junior medical assistant or just a warm body playing the role—she knew nothing. It almost sounded as if this was her first job; one that she did not want. She did not seem to be interested in working at all for that matter—something I would soon find out first hand.

What perfect timing—my hot flashes were now getting worse. I was not trying to be a pain in the rear, but I did need and requested for my blankets to be removed and replaced—off and on again—as my hot flashes dictated. Whenever possible, I would ask my family to help as opposed to calling for the nurse to help. I tried to resist asking—but the hot flashes made it unbearable to be covered with blankets. And when the hot flashes subsided I would get the chills and need the blankets back on. I was miserable.

Anyway, I will call this young medical assistant (giving her the benefit of the doubt), Daughter Dearest. She was barely in her early twenties and was more interested in flirting with the male nurses in the CCU than actually assisting patients. Oh—and the constant giggling, or should I say cackling, really tried my patience. In fact, I was her only patient and she still did not want anything to do with her job—hello, caring for me. Although early on she did stop by a few times to respond to my pleas for water, ice-chips, and blankets moved on and off.

When it was finally time for my blood pressure to be taken—Daughter Dearest had no idea how to take someone's blood pressure.

So, yet another nurse had to come over and teach her how. Instead of the regular removable arm wrap, she was given a plastic blood pressure sleeve to use as a substitute. I'd never seen such a thing before and I will never forget it either. After she was finished, she was instructed to remove the plastic sleeve. Thereafter, she was further instructed to repeat the procedure, monitoring my blood pressure every hour and recording the results.

An hour later she was back, armed with the plastic blood pressure sleeve. Knowing that her instructor had since left, this time after taking my blood pressure, Daughter Dearest would leave the plastic sleeve in place. It covered my entire upper arm; talk about hot flashes going into overdrive.

"Excuse me—could you please come back and remove this plastic sleeve?" I begged. "It's very uncomfortable and it is making me miserably hot."

"I will in a minute," Daughter Dearest answered, obviously annoyed.

"Excuse me—please—my hot flashes are going into overdrive?" I pleaded again after getting no response.

Moments later, still no response. I knew this was going to be a losing battle. Weak and tired I decided not to bother. Instead, I endured the accelerated hot flashes and tried to get some sleep.

While in the CCU, I was in a standard hospital bed, its head backed up against a table against a single wall. The bed was surrounded by curtains, which hung from tracks on the ceiling and could be slid open or closed. My bed was located just outside the nurses' station. Throughout the day, I could hear Daughter Dearest with the male nurses, carrying on as if on a hot date. But as long as she was assisting me when I needed help, I didn't really care.

After a few rounds of asking Daughter Dearest to assist me with the basics—water, ice-chips, food, and the occasional on and off move of my blankets—I realized she was no longer coming around to help me. In fact, several hours had passed since she last took my blood pressure. Yet I could still hear her at the nurses' station—carrying on with the male nurses—just outside my room.

"Excuse me. Can I please get some more ice-chips—my hot flashes are killing me?"

She ignored me.

So again, a little louder I asked, "Excuse me. Can I please get some more ice-chips?"

Again, I was ignored.

Now I was pissed off! I did not ask to be there! I was still there because something—obviously—went wrong with respect to my "routine hysterectomy!" Yet I could hear Daughter Dearest flirting away with the male nurses at the nurses' station. She couldn't be so dumb as to think keeping my curtains closed would silence me—I thought to myself. So I got very loud.

"Excuse me!" I demanded. "I need some assistance—NOW!"

It worked. She opened my curtains and came into my area. However, to my dismay, she only did so to tell me off.

"I do not plan on having a nursing career," she ranted. "And I don't like this temporary assignment. So I am no longer going to respond to you."

Seemingly proud of herself, she abruptly left my area, flinging the curtains closed behind her.

I was INFURIATED! At this point I didn't even care about the hot flashes or the pain I was in. THIS WAS WAR!

"OPEN MY CURTAINS RIGHT NOW!!" I yelled.

If she was going to flirt and ignore me, I was going to watch her doing it. I figured I could make my point that way.

Then without a word, she pushed opened my curtains but only ever so slightly—she was playing with me.

Screw this!

"OPEN MY CURTAINS ALL THE WAY!!!" I yelled even louder.

My tone must have scared her as she was back to push open my curtains—all the way this time.

Nevertheless, I apparently hadn't scared her enough, because now no one was assisting me. And all I wanted was some ice-chips to help manage my hot flashes.

With my curtains now opened—all the way—I looked around the CCU. It did not appear that there were any other patients in the CCU—only the three of them and myself. I was feeling defeated and miserable and my left leg was killing me. Instinctively, I wanted to fight back—so I did.

"I want to see a doctor?" I asked calmly—a new approach I thought.

"The on-call doctor will not be in until this evening," one of the male nurse's replied.

I was continuing to get more and more frustrated. I was just lying there in the CCU—helpless—and I still had not spoken to a doctor since Friday. Then I had an "Ah-ha!" moment. It was only Sunday and of course there were no doctors on staff other than the phantom on-call doctor.

I had no idea what they were doing with me. I didn't even know when or if I would ever be released from the CCU. Okay, so I was exaggerating again. And now I had been sentenced with this medical assistant from hell, Daughter Dearest. I felt like I was in a bad movie that was never going to end.

Finally fed up, early evening, I asked for the head nurse in charge. God knows I couldn't find a doctor. At first I was ignored—of course. So I began to get louder and louder. Now I sounded like the patient from hell—but it worked.

Suddenly, the head nurse came rushing in as if with a purpose. Then as if nothing had happened, she told me it was time to move me to an inpatient room. She looked like she was straight out of the 1950's, probably middle-aged, and had a Laverne and Shirley like personality. She wore an oversized white coat—unbuttoned—over her clothes. Her thick shoulder length hair had obviously been dyed a deep auburn red color and it was styled with thick bangs and a very distinctive 1950's flip at the ends. She looked like she was right out of a Happy Days Hollywood sitcom scene.

She ordered one of the male nurses to assist her and together they began disconnecting the machines and equipment I had been hooked up to—with the exception of the IV rack which would follow me—still firmly connected to the central line implanted in my chest.

First, they disconnected the epidural for the first time since my original surgery—four days ago. Next they took me off the oxygen I had been on. After that my catheter bag was thrown between my legs on top of the bed. My overnight bag was placed in my lap as well. Then, the infamous plastic blood pressure sleeve was finally removed from my arm. And last, the painful sequential compression devices were removed from my lower legs.

Moments later, I was whisked off to an inpatient room—but the saga wouldn't end there. On the way to the room, I started crying as I was now in extreme pain—the pain in my left leg was actually in my left foot, ankle, and leg. The pain level went through the roof to a threshold of ten. (In a hospital setting, they measure your threshold of pain from one to ten. One being almost no pain and ten being the highest level of pain — which is pretty unbearable.) I was beside myself. I was living a nightmare from which I could not escape.

Apparently, the epidural, after being removed had quickly thereafter worn off. Thus, it was no longer masking the severity of the pain in my left foot, ankle, and leg. I mean it was agonizing! I couldn't control my emotions.

No one knew what to do or what was happening. Several doctors came to my rescue, ordering the nursing staff to immediately get a hold of my doctor—Dr. X.

Then they tried to wheel me into an inpatient room, but it was occupied. So then they wheeled me into a temporary room until the new inpatient room they wanted to put me in was ready. However, I guess that room was not happening either, so they wheeled me back out into the corridor near the administration desk where I'd started from—and where I was left to wait for Dr. X to arrive.

Blood Clots

Up until now, I had been having very light conversations with the God. I knew He was busy and with His support I believed that if I was well enough to get out of the CCU that I would be well on my road to a complete recovery. My children were still on vacation and didn't know I was even in the hospital. Nonetheless, unbeknownst to me, my nightmare was only in the beginning scenes.

Now, I was begging and pleading with God to help me. I would do anything he wanted. I just wanted to be given a sign and be told what to do to make my pain go away. Then, a nurse kindly offered to give me Vicodin to relieve some of the pain I was in while I waited for Dr. X.

"No!" I shrieked.

"Vicodin makes me nauseous," I whined. "Dr. X had previously prescribed Vicodin and it made me sick."

"Get her a Percocet," another nurse suggested.

I took the Percocet and shortly thereafter—it at least got me off the moon—the pain was a bit bearable.

When Dr. X finally arrived, he was shocked to see me just lying there in the hallway in front of the administration desk.

"What is she doing out here in the hallway?" he demanded.

He was angry but he treated me with his usual warm bedside manner. He started to probe my left ankle and foot. Next, he ordered the nurse to get him a portable Doppler machine. Then he, along with an orderly who was pushing my bed, escorted me to an inpatient room down the hall.

Just as we had gotten situated in the room, another orderly entered the room, pushing the bed of yet another patient. Dr. X stopped him immediately and ordered him to take his patient to another room. Knowing what I had been through, he wanted me to have a private room. I was feeling pretty special at that point—anything to get my mind off the pain.

Moments later, a nurse came in with the portable Doppler machine and handed it to Dr. X. He turned on the machine and began to probe my left foot, ankle, and leg. The portable Doppler machine preliminarily indicated little to no pulse in my left foot, ankle, and leg. Immediately he and the nurse suspected blood clots.

Now my husband and parents had just arrived too. They had left for dinner while I was being moved from the CCU—and this time they had my oldest son with them. Again, my husband and parents had no idea what was happening.

"Hi," I groaned, obviously in a lot of pain.

"Hi mom, I can't believe you are still in the hospital," my son said while giving me a hug.

"Now what?" my mom asked warily.

"When they took me off the epidural the pain in my left foot, ankle, and leg quickly shot to ten," I explained.

"I can't believe this," my dad said, grinding his teeth.

"They brought in a portable Doppler machine and confirmed that there is little to no pulse in my left foot, ankle, and leg," I continued. "They suspect blood clots."

Tears started to run down my face as I was scared all over again.

"Is there anything I can do sweetie?" my husband asked cautiously.

"Nothing," I answered. "They tried to give me Vicodin, but I told them no. So they gave me a Percocet instead—that at least brought my pain down to a six or seven."

Next, Dr. X arranged for another test to take place in the hospital's Doppler lab, which was equipped with advanced high-tech Doppler equipment. During my test, a lab technician, who I will call Hotlips was present to operate the equipment and assist the doctor performing the exam. Then he called in two vascular surgeons, who I will call, Drs. Obnoxious and TooCool to do the exam. Dr. Obnoxious had "hospital privileges" at another hospital and Dr. TooCool had "hospital privileges" yet at a third hospital. Drs. Obnoxious and TooCool were at Dr. X's hospital by invitation.[11]

Dr. Obnoxious was the first to arrive. While Dr. X was briefing him—outside my room—a nurse appeared and told the two doctors that Hotlips was in the lab and ready. I was then wheeled from my room down the hall for my exam. On the way, I was introduced to Dr.

47

Obnoxious and together the two doctors pushed my bed into the Doppler lab. Afterwards, Dr. X and the nurse dismissed themselves.

Once in the lab—at first sight—Dr. Obnoxious was smitten with Hotlips. All focus was off me and he was now flagrantly flirting with her. In spite of this, she didn't seem to mind at all. They continued on—hence, the names Hotlips and Dr. Obnoxious—while screening my blood flow and pulse with the stationary Doppler equipment. It was as if I wasn't even there—I was just some sort of lab rat they were performing random tests on. Amazing! I thought.

After the exam, Dr. Obnoxious confirmed with Dr. X that he too believed I had blood clots in my left leg preventing blood flow. He immediately suspected that a suture was causing the blockage.

They were especially concerned because they did not yet know whether the blood clots were arterial (in my arteries) or intravenous (in my veins). If arterial, I was assured the blood clots would not move past my limbs and would not be life threatening; however, if they were intravenous, the blood clots could travel up my veins and upon reaching my heart could kill me. Later, I would research deep vein thrombosis (DVT) and peripheral artery disease (PAD) in which I have provided my findings herein.[12/13]

Dr. TooCool had now arrived. Drs. X and Obnoxious brought him up-to-speed with what was happening. Together, each of the doctors agreed that a CT scan using contrast dye should be performed to further confirm their conclusions. Dr. X thereafter set the motions in place to arrange such a test.

Again, I was returned to my private inpatient room. My husband, parents, and son were all there waiting for my return and diagnosis. Dr. X introduced Drs. Obnoxious and TooCool to my family. They discussed their preliminary findings and explained that I would be undergoing a CT scan test momentarily.[14]

As the doctors were finishing up with their update to my family, they again, were interrupted. One of the nurses and a lab technician had arrived to take me to the CT lab. So off I went—another test—another diagnosis.

As I was being wheeled through the hallways and corridors, I finally had a chance to look around—the hospital wing that I was being wheeled through oddly seemed disserted. On one side of the hallway, I could see workstations but no staff. On the other side, I could see large letters sprawled along the wall that spelt out "O N C O L O G Y."

"Why is the Oncology ward so disserted?" I asked.

"The hospital use to have an Oncology department, but they shut it down," the lab technician answered. "This hospital is now being used primarily by OB/GYN's delivering babies and performing other female routine surgeries."

"Where is the newborn ward, then?" I asked.

"Down the hall and to the right is delivery, and further down the hall is the newborn ward," he answered.

When we arrived at the CT lab, a second technician joined in to help me out of my bed and onto the CT scanner bed. Surprisingly, it was a very long and narrow bed. And I wondered, "How would a larger person manage to lie on the bed without falling off?"

More needles I thought—as they prepared the back of my right hand to be shot up with contrast dye. I watched in silence. I was told that I would feel warm sensations fill my body and that the whole procedure would be done in minutes.

Then, as I lied there, the bed began to move backwards into what looked like an enclosed tube. Though, pleasantly surprised, there was no closure on the other side. It was as if my head had just gone through a large machine collar. After a few minutes, the procedure was over and I was returned to my bed and again wheeled back through the maze of halls to my room.

Within the hour, the doctors were back in my room. They had received the CT scan images, reviewed them, and had confirmed their earlier findings. Though I was not shown the images, Dr. Obnoxious insisted the findings indicated a suture around my iliac leg artery. (I felt a bit relieved that they had confirmed that the blood clots were arterial and non-life threatening.) As Dr. TooCool concurred with Dr. Obnoxious' findings, Dr. X remained speechless but cooperative.

Drs. Obnoxious and TooCool agreed that surgery would be required to break the suture and hopefully restore my blood flow and that they were both willing to do it. They warned, however, that since it had been four days since my original surgery that the damage to my leg was probably already done.

Next they strategized on how best to restore the blood flow in my leg after the suture was broken. Dr. TooCool took charge over Drs. X and Obnoxious and suggested an arterial femoro-femoral bypass graft. Both doctors agreed with Dr. TooCool that this would be the best solution.

Shortly thereafter, an argument ensued, as Drs. Obnoxious and TooCool refused to perform the surgery in Dr. X's hospital. The three doctors began to argue, right in front of me as if I wasn't even there. Apparently, Dr. X did not have "hospital privileges" in either of the other two hospitals that Drs. Obnoxious and TooCool had. Finally, they resolved that Dr. TooCool would do the surgery at his hospital.

I guess I had no say—no one was even paying attention to me. Nevertheless, I was relieved that Dr. TooCool would be doing my surgery. I didn't care much for Dr. Obnoxious. His previous actions spoke volumes and he had lost all credibility with me.

After Drs. TooCool and Obnoxious left, Dr. X stayed to further brief my family and me on next steps. This would be the third surgery I would have to endure. And since it had been decided that Dr. TooCool would be performing the surgery, he would be doing so outside of Dr. X's hospital. This meant Dr. X would have to arrange transportation to get me to and from the hospitals.

"I would like to immediately start her on a regimen of Heparin," Dr. X said. "Heparin is a commonly used blood thinner, used by physicians to prevent excessive clotting. Thinning the blood prevents new clots from forming and prevents the enlargement of existing ones."

"How long will I need to be on the Heparin?" I asked.

"Just until your surgery," he answered.

"Is it just a pill?" I asked.

"No—it will be a daily shot," he said.

The nurse had now walked in with the syringe of Heparin and a sterilized wipe in her hand. Dr. X retrieved the syringe from the nurse along with the sterilized wipe. He then cleaned a small area on my abdomen and administered the shot. Surprisingly, it didn't hurt.

"Tomorrow morning, I will show you how-to give yourself a daily shot," he said nonchalantly.

"Wait—wait—why would I be giving myself the shots?" I asked.

"If you are released from the hospital before your upcoming surgery, you will need to administer your own shots from home," he answered.

"Why would I be released from the hospital?" I asked. "I have no use of my left leg without the surgery. I thought surgery would be immediate."

"More than likely the surgery will be soon," he answered. "But . . . first . . . we have to get you strong enough to endure a third surgery— the timing will depend on Dr. TooCool's schedule as well. We should know more in a couple of days."

I was speechless. I hated needles and the thought of injecting myself made me cringe even more. Nonetheless, at this point, I was helpless and I had no use of my left leg without this regimen. By now, I was exhausted—and cold again—so I asked my husband to help me wrap myself in blankets before I dozed off.

Confessions

I was startled and awakened from a sound sleep. It was dark and I was scared. I heard something coming down the hall—it sounded like a train roaring towards me. I knew the back wall of my room was an external wall of the building as I had a window on that wall. I wondered if my room was next to train tracks—the sound was so loud and I could hear it getting louder by the second. I felt petrified. I had goose bumps and chills up and down my spine. My heart was racing—but I couldn't move. Then suddenly, the noise abruptly stopped. Next I heard my husband and a nurse talking.

Evidently, this warm-hearted nurse, found my husband in my room sleeping in an upright chair. She woke him and asked for his assistance—she had found an old-style heavy-duty metal hideaway bed in storage for him to sleep on. This was what was causing all the noise, the bed rattling as they pushed it down the hospital corridor. Unbeknownst to my husband and I, this would be the first night of many more to come, where he would stay with me in the hospital overnight. He would read the last book in the Harry Potter series and then get through six David Morrell paperbacks before my nightmare would be over.

As I listened, I pretended to be asleep. They were trying to be careful not to disturb me. Although, pointless I thought, as I was sure they had woken up anyone who was in the hospital. Finally, she handed him blankets and he snuggled in.

Throughout the night, I would awake to my husband's snoring and the nurse, whom would be peering from the doorway of my room watching. I was not sure if she was watching me or my husband, but to me, she felt more like a guardian angel—it was comforting.

Day 5 - Monday

Always an early riser, and apparently Dr. X was too, I woke at about 6:00 a.m. My husband must have left earlier in the morning—for home and then work—since he was now gone. When Dr. X arrived, he was wearing his jogging clothes. He made himself comfortable and sat on the bed my husband had been sleeping on as if he was sitting on a couch.

"Good morning—you're awake," he said.

"Yes—I am typically an early riser," I replied.

"I was on my morning jog when I decided to drop by and check on you before beginning my day at the office," he said.

I nodded.

"Lately—jogging is the only thing in my life that makes me happy," he said. "It gives me a sense of empowerment."

I listened.

"At home—I am the only male," he continued while fumbling with his hands. "I have a wife and daughters. My youngest is about to graduate from college—so soon I will be done raising my children."

I was starting to feel like a therapist. He had not asked me a single question about me or how I was feeling. He just kept rambling on about his personal life.

"My life is very lonely," he rambled. "It seems like the women in my life just push me aside. I feel like an outsider in my own home—my wife and daughters rarely pay any attention to me."

Are you kidding me? Was this guy trying to make me feel sorry for him? I was the one who had just gone through two surgeries because of a botched hysterectomy that he had performed! And I still needed a third surgery!

"Anyway, jogging gives me solitude—it's the only time I really feel empowered," he continued. "Tonight, my wife and daughters and I are going to dinner for a family function that I need to attend."

"Okay," I said.

"Please, let me give you my personal cell phone number," he said, almost apologetically as he wrote down his number on a piece of paper and handed it to me.

"Feel free to call me for any reason," he added.

"Thank you," I said.

I had started feeling uncomfortable as he went on and on about more of his personal life. I couldn't figure out where he was coming from. For example, was his guilty conscious getting the best of him potentially causing a confession—undiagnosed endometriosis, botched hysterectomy, leaving me to bleed to death, line misplacement causing me to stop breathing? Or was he trying to win me over for a cover up?

Was he hitting on me? Who knows—but none of his rambling seemed appropriate to me.

"So what should I expect with respect to my recovery?" I asked—anything to change the subject to me.

"Well, you have already been through two surgeries and with one surgery it takes the body a full year to completely recoup the electrolytes lost during that surgery," he explained.

"What are electrolytes?" I asked.

"Electrolytes are minerals that carry an electric charge, they are found in the blood and other body fluids," he said. "It is important that the balance of electrolytes in your body be maintained. They affect the body's water retention, blood pH, muscle action, and other important processes. For example, you lose electrolytes when you sweat, so they must be replenished by drinking lots of fluids."

Enough with the science of electrolytes[15] I thought. I was getting irritable and very bored.

"So—I guess that means right now—it would take two full years for my body to recover from the surgeries I have already been through?" I interrupted.

"It could—but it's not always that simple—one plus one does not necessarily equal two," he replied.

"What is post-traumatic stress disorder that Dr. Y warned me about when I was in the CCU?" I asked, changing the subject once again.

"PTSD is a type of anxiety problem," he answered. "It can develop after your safety or life is threatened—or after you experience or see a traumatic event, things such as: natural disasters, rape, severe car crash, war, etc."

"Okay," I said.

"I think what Dr. Y was referring to was with respect to the complications you experienced during your surgeries," he continued. "These kinds of events can make you feel very afraid or helpless. People with PTSD can have trouble coping with and getting over traumatic events and can often feel the effects for months or even years afterward."

Again, I was bored.

"What about my bandages?" I interrupted again. "They have not been changed in two days."

I was concerned about infections.

He then stood up and walked over to my bedside. "Let's take a look," he said, while he removed the gauze that was taped to my body as bandages.

This was the first time I had seen my incisions and all the staples—the staples were huge and looked like heavy-duty metal staples construction workers would use. My abdomen looked grossly deformed. All the same, I was exhausted and felt like I needed to "play nice" if I wanted to get out of this nightmare and become whole again.

"Your wounds will heal faster if they are exposed to the air and covered only by your hospital gown," he said. "I will instruct the nurses not to redress your incisions anymore."

Disturbingly, though he had removed my bandages, he made no attempt to clean my wounds or even tell a nurse to do so. Instead, my incisions were now exposed to the hospital air and whatever else my surrounding environment had to offer. To make matters worse, my incisions were beginning to show signs of infection in several areas. I was concerned and nervous all over again.

Then he said, in a very matter of fact tone like it was no big deal. "You'll probably need to go to wound therapy anyway."

Immediately, more alarms were going off in my head.

"I will be back later to check in," he said as he walked out the door.

Our conversation left me cold, weak, and trembling. In an effort to get warm, I wrapped one of my blankets around my head and fussed with several more until I was completely covered—only my face peering out. I was finally warm and able to ponder for the first time.

I knew I would have to endure a third surgery; so again, I turned to God and had a deep conversation with him. I explained that I still had things to do. I had two more sons to finish bringing up. And so, I asked for strength, telling Him I would do my part . . . When we were finished with our chat, I felt better. Knowing intuitively that sleep was the best healer—I closed my eyes and fell back to sleep.

Doctors Protecting Doctors

Several hours later I awoke again. I needed to go to the bathroom to go poop. However, I had not been out of bed for five days—this would be the first time that I would try to get out of bed. So I decided not to be stupid and called for a nurse to help me to my private bathroom a few feet away from my bed.

Upon arrival of the nurse, I explained that I needed to go poop. She asked me to wait while she retrieved a walker. When she returned, with the support of the walker, she assisted me out of bed. My arms were shaking violently as I struggled to hold myself up and walk the few short steps to the bathroom. I could not believe how weak I was. It was as if I needed to learn how to sit, stand, and walk all over again.

As I finished pooping I could feel that my strength was deteriorating. Again, I called the nurse and asked for her assistance so that I could get back into my bed. A minute or so later, the nurse appeared back in my room, but this time she had a grave expression on her face.

She looked at me and said, "Getting out of bed the first time is the hardest thing you'll do. If you get right back into bed now—you won't want to get out of bed again."

I believe this was the most important advice anyone had ever given me. I felt like I was going to die—I was so weak and sick. Nevertheless, I took this nurse's wisdom and again with her assistance—and the support of the walker—I made it to the chair facing the end of my bed. It took all my strength to get there.

Then, I sat there and this, too, was so hard to do. Again, I felt like I was going to die all over again. But I knew I had to do this if I wanted to get better and out of this hospital. So I sat as the nurse re-wrapped me—in warm blankets this time—and then left.

Moments later, my parents arrived. They were pleasantly surprised and hopeful to see me sitting in a chair and out of my bed. As we caught up, I told them Dr. X had come by earlier that morning and removed my bandages. I also told them about my first bowel movement. Then I complained that I was hungry and that the hospital food was horrible.

My mother intuitively got my cue and offered to bring back whatever I wanted. So I asked for some Captain Crunch Berry cereal, milk, and a bowl and spoon. And for the first time, I was delighted about something.

Twenty minutes later, I asked to be assisted back to bed.

My kids were expected back from their vacation today and I was anxious to see them. So I asked my parents to contact their dad on my behalf and to tell him that I was in the hospital asking for the kids. Regardless of how this would end—still scared about my impending

60

third surgery—I wanted to see my boys. In addition to missing them, I knew I owed them an explanation and I wanted to reassure them that I was going to be all right.

Other than my immediate family, whom lived in town, I had asked for no visitors. I didn't even want my brothers flying in from out of state even though they had offered. I peculiarly felt their presence of doing so would send a death sentence message to my body—and I wasn't ready to leave this world. I also asked that no flowers be sent. I didn't want anything around me that could signify a premature death—flowers never lasted me more than a week.

Dr. X returned, now in his scrubs. My mom had left for work and it was just my dad and I.

"Good morning," he said.

"Good morning," I replied.

My dad silently greeted Dr. X with a smile and a nod.

"As promised, I have brought with me your Heparin shot," he said. "I'm going to show you how to inject yourself."

"Okay," I replied.

"You're right handed, correct?" he asked.

"Yes," I replied.

"I want you to pinch a small roll of skin from your abdomen with your left hand and hold it," he instructed.

I fumbled around with my gown, exposing only the top part of my abdomen as I didn't want to embarrass my dad or myself. Then, following Dr. X's instructions, I pinched a small roll of skin from my abdomen with my left hand and held it.

"Now—using your right hand—wipe it clean with this sterilized wipe," he instructed, handing me the pad. "I'm going to hand you the syringe—but before I do—I want you to notice this small air bubble at the top. You will need to hold the needle upright—then press gently on the plunger until a drop of the Heparin is released. This will force the air bubble out so you don't inject yourself with it."

As he handed me the syringe with Heparin, I did as he instructed—holding the needle upright, forcing out a drop of Heparin.

"Next, you want to quickly stick yourself with the needle in the sterilized area, while still pinching your abdomen and squeezing the Heparin from the syringe," he instructed.

I handled it flawlessly. My dad thought I was brave—he too does not like needles.

Dr. X then left my room.

A short time later, Dr. Lifesaver arrived in my room. This was the first time I had ever seen Dr. Lifesaver from what I could recall. He was gorgeous! Tall and slender, he wore black slacks with a striking olive green shirt. His shoes were polished and he looked flawless.

"Good morning," he said.

"Good morning," I replied.

"Good morning," dad replied. Dad had obviously met Dr. Lifesaver before and recognized him.

"How are you feeling today?" Dr. Lifesaver asked.

"Better than last night," I replied. "They seem to have me on an every four hour regimen of Percocet which is keeping my pain down."

"Let's take a look at your incisions," he said as he glanced over at my dad.

My dad immediately got the hint and excused himself from the room. He said he was going to step out for a while and get some breakfast. He would be back in an hour.

"I know we haven't officially met—but I was the doctor that joined Dr. X performing your emergency surgery," he said.

"Yes—and from what I understand—you saved my life," I said.

Dr. Lifesaver smiled with a charming smirk on his face.

"I'm a cancer reconstructive surgeon and unlike an OB/GYN surgeon I can work above the bikini line," he said as he began examining my incisions. "Accordingly, I made a vertical incision from the center of your horizontal incisions up your abdomen—so that I could open you up wider to see where the bleeding was coming from."

Strange, it seemed like this was a critical point that Dr. Lifesaver wanted me to remember. I distinctively got the impression that we were having this discussion as some sort of defense. Perhaps it was to confirm that the area where my leg appeared to be sutured, he never accessed.

"After I made the incision and opened you up—I was able to stop your bleeding," he continued. "However, I noticed that your ureter tubes and bladder were in very bad shape—the tissue was severely scarred by the endometriosis—so I went ahead and made the necessary repairs. In doing so I placed a ureteral stent in your ureters to keep your ureter tubes open.

"What are these little bulbs hanging from each side of me?" I asked.

"Those are called 'JP drains,' they're commonly used after more invasive surgeries. They're similar to the bulb at the end of a turkey baser. We squeeze the air out before they are attached—this creates suction which draws out excess fluid from the abdominal cavity."

"Thank you," I interjected. "I know I had been recently experiencing frequent urination but could hardly pee at all—that was the symptom that prompted the findings that I needed a hysterectomy."

Dr. Lifesaver looked at me with pause.

"So, if you had not made the repairs to my bladder, I would have required another surgery anyway?" I asked.

"Yes—your bladder was in very bad shape," he answered.

"How long do I have to have the stent and these bags hanging off my sides?" I asked, flipping one with my hand.

"The bags and stent are temporary," he answered. "We will remove the bags when it looks like there is no more drainage. However, as far as the stent goes, I would like to leave that in place for at least the next four months."

"How long will the staples need to be in me?" I asked.

"Your incisions are still fresh and I can see some oozing—so I don't want to remove them yet," he answered.

"Dr. X took my bandages off earlier this morning," I volunteered looking for confirmation. "He said he did not want my incisions redressed and that it would be better to keep them exposed."

Dr. Lifesaver just stared at me without commenting. I could see in his eyes that he had so much to say but wouldn't.

So I decided to spare him and broke the silence.

"Thank you Dr. Lifesaver," I said gratefully. "Thank you so much for everything—I really appreciate everything you have done."

"I will be back in a couple of days to check in on you again," he confirmed and then dismissed himself.

Next, Dr. TooCool arrived. It was like I had a revolving door—one doctor right after the other. He, too, was dressed to the nines. He was wearing black slacks and a stunning royal blue shirt. I was very impressed that these two doctors (Drs. Lifesaver and TooCool) took dressing for success seriously—something I was very familiar with.

"Good morning," he said energetically.

64

"Good morning," I replied with a smile.

"How are you feeling today?" he asked.

"Good—I guess," I replied. "Dr. Lifesaver was just here. He told me more about the emergency surgery."

"So how is your leg today?" he asked.

"Pretty much the same—a lot of pain—but Percocet is helping," I answered.

"I just checked my surgery schedule and I have an opening on Wednesday at noon," he said.

"Great!" I said excitedly.

He smiled, noticeably seeing that my spirits were upbeat and positive. Something he seemed very pleased by.

"However—before going into surgery— I want to schedule another CT scan at my hospital," he continued.

"Okay," I said.

"I will schedule it for 10:00 a.m. that morning," he continued. "That should give me enough time to review the images and determine whether or not breaking the suture will restore the blood flow in your leg."

"Okay," I said cautiously.

"If breaking the suture does not sufficiently restore the blood flow to your leg—then I recommend an arterial femoro-femoral bypass graft," he said.

"What is a femoro-femoral bypass graft?" I asked.

"It's like implanting a new road connecting two existing roads in your groin area," he explained. "The fem-fem bypass will reroute the flow of blood from your right femoral artery to your left femoral artery."

"I trust you and I appreciate that you are willing to do the surgery," I said. "So yes—whatever you suggest—I will be fine with."

"Great—then I will let Dr. X know our plans and ask him to make the transportation arrangements for Wednesday morning at 9:00 a.m.," he concluded.

"Thank you," I said.

He smiled and then left the room.

Guess what? You guessed it—Dr. X was back.

"Well—I see you and Dr. TooCool have just had a chat and that he will be doing your next surgery in a couple of days," he said.

"Yes," I smiled—happy that things were moving along.

Then, in walked my dad and mom. Dr. X and I updated them about my upcoming surgery with Dr. TooCool.

"How will she get to the other hospital?" my mom asked.

"She can go with you or her husband—or we could arrange for an ambulance," Dr. X answered.

"What if something were to happen?" my mother asked. "She can barely walk and is in a very fragile state. We can't take that kind of responsibility. You guys did this to her—you need to continue her care until she is well."

"Not a problem—I will write the orders for hospital administration to arrange for an ambulance," Dr. X agreed.

"Will she be coming back to this hospital?" my mom asked.

"Yes—she can leave her personal belongings here. She will be transported back here after her surgery," he answered.

My parents were speechless and didn't have any more questions, but both were very skeptical.

Dr. X nodded and left my room.

Immediately, my parents and I joined in a make shift huddle. I told them that as soon as I was out of Dr. X's hospital, under no circumstance was I ever returning. They agreed.

Late that afternoon, my oldest son came to visit me. He was shocked and couldn't believe that his mother was yet still in the hospital. I reassured him that things were going to be fine. Nonetheless, he was very nervous about me going through a third surgery so soon after the last two.

I explained that if I didn't have the surgery, I would lose the use of my leg and possibly be in a wheelchair. More importantly, if I didn't take care of my leg now, I could possibly lose my leg altogether. I explained that I was doing a lot of sleeping as I knew from experience now that sleeping was healing.

Speaking of which, I was once again exhausted—so I mentioned to my dad and son that I was going to take a nap. My mother had already gone back to work as she had earlier stopped by on her lunch hour. Like good soldiers, my dad and son sat there quietly as if it was their watch.

As I was sure they were both bored out of their minds, I handed them the remote control for the television before dozing off. I still hadn't had any energy to read or watch television—only to sleep. And, lucky for me, I was one of those fortunate individuals who could sleep through just about anything.

Finally, that evening, I would need to put my best face forward and make things appear less grim—when my ex-husband showed up with my two younger sons. When they arrived, they too were shocked and dismayed by my appearance. I had always been a healthy active petite young mother—but now, I looked broken.

Yet, at that moment, I could see in their eyes that they had mixed emotions. While they were very frightened for me on one hand, they were very angry on the other. They had not been told about any of my surgeries or anything I was going through until now. Later, we would have this discussion, and we would make a pact that from then on they would be told everything—full disclosure—before anyone goes to the hospital again.

Once again, I felt as if the life was being (temporarily) drained out of me. I had not been bathed in five days and my hair felt like it was glued to the top of my head. I had just been through two surgeries and now I had to prepare for a third surgery—at yet another hospital. Thus, I cut the visit short and told them, "mom was tired and needed to sleep." I hugged and kissed them both good night.

Summer Heat

Another restless night, it was only 11:00 p.m. and I was awake again and miserable. In addition to the pain caused by my wounds—clearly infected from the staples, sutures, and who knows what else—my hot flashes were getting stronger again. It was summer and the hospital itself seemed like it was ninety degrees. I couldn't take it anymore, so I pushed my call button and called for the nurse.

"Hi, you called?" a young voice responded.

"Yes—I feel like I am melting, my pain level feels like it is getting worse, and I am absolutely miserable," I whined.

"I know—you've been through a lot," she nurtured.

She must have read my chart. Probably not much else to do I thought—on the night shift—when most patients were sleeping.

"Is there any way you can turn up the air-conditioner?" I begged.

"No—the thermostat is pre-set," she said. "But let me first see if I can find you a fan to help with the heat."

Moments later, she returned with a giant fan. The fan was at least forty-eight inches wide and stood on a stand six feet tall—that quickly put a smile on my face. Then I looked over at my husband. He was sleeping peacefully, completely oblivious to anything happening around him.

"Hopefully this will help," she said, as she finished positioning the fan, and then turned it on.

"Thank you so much," I said gratefully.

"Now you mentioned you were in more pain than usual," she said.

"Yes—my wounds seem to be killing me—especially this pain deep on one side of my pelvis," I explained, pointing to my side. "And on top of that I am feeling nauseous."

"Well, looking at your chart I can see that you had your last Percocet three hours ago, but I will go ahead and give you another one now," she said.

"I will also get you something for your nausea," she continued as she hurried out of the room.

A few minutes later she returned with the Percocet and a new drug—Protonix—for my nausea.

"Here you go," she said, handing me my glass of water along with the pills.

"Thank you," I said as I quickly washed down the Percocet—followed by the Protonix.

Then she disappeared.

About ten minutes later, I was pleasantly surprised that the nausea had gone away and I was able to fall back to sleep.

Day 6 - Tuesday

I woke up and thanked God for another day. With my new friend, the large fan, my hot flashes seemed more manageable—but now I was starving. I knew I needed to eat; yet nothing on the hospital menu sounded remotely appetizing. I turned to the cereal that I had asked my mom to bring in and prepared a bowl. After a couple of bites, this too made me nauseous—but I knew I had to eat. I needed nourishment if I expected to get better, so I forced whatever I could down.

At about 9:00 a.m. my dad was back—great guy, quiet, and always comforting. I guess it was his watch this morning. My husband and mom were both at work. Meanwhile, I was anxious about tomorrow's surgery and still in a lot of pain.

In addition to my surgical wounds, I continued to suffer from large blisters on my legs. It appeared on one leg that something must have burned me—most likely caused during my surgeries. I had terrible bruising on my neck from where they had tried—unsuccessfully—to implant a "central line." (The "central line" would be used to administer drugs through instead of continued needle punctures in my arms. It would also be used to monitor specific vital signs.) I also had more bruising on my upper chest, where they—successfully— implanted the "central line," and where it was still firmly implanted. My arms felt like hard baseballs in the inner elbow area and were numb from all the needles I had been stuck with—I looked like a battered woman.[16]

On top of everything else, even though I had no energy, I was now bored out of my mind. I could tell my dad was bored as well. And so, I told him I wanted to take a nap and he could go. I assured him I would be fine—and I was sure he was relieved to hear my words.

71

Okay—now that dad was gone—I had a plan. Since I had forced some food down, I was no longer hungry. Now, to tackle my hygiene, I asked the nurse to bring me some bathing supplies—any bathing supplies. I had been able to get to and from the bathroom by myself during my last several trips. So I figured if I could sit in front of the bathroom sink, I could give myself a sponge bath—and potentially wash my hair.

Well, the nurse returned with soap, toothpaste, and a couple of towels. No shampoo or razors were available—had I known I was going to have such a long hospital stay, I would have packed such necessary items. As a result, a sponge bath it was.

Next I asked for a clean gown. Then I brushed my teeth and was finally beginning to feel halfway human again. Except, these seemingly minor tasks had now taken a toll on me and I was exhausted once again—so I retreated back to bed.

For the rest of the day I would do a lot of soul searching, praying, and napping. I made a lot of promises to God—promises that I knew I could keep. Although I was very nervous about having a third surgery so soon—I knew I had to keep my anxiety at bay and remain calm. I found resting and being calm very healing and peaceful.

In addition, I knew I had to keep my excitement of getting the heck out of Dr. X's hospital in check. While the nurses handled the final details of my upcoming ambulance transportation—for the next day and return—I stayed silent. I had already had discussions with my family. I had PPO insurance and could go wherever I wanted. And there was no way, after "getting out of Dodge" tomorrow morning that I was ever coming back to Dr. X's hospital again.

That evening, my husband returned—as he always had following a quick trip home after work. But this evening would be different. I was still not eating much because I could not stand the hospital food. The hospital had a single kitchen ran by a husband and wife team and a couple of vending machines—nothing seemed appetizing to me.

For these reasons, I justified my next actions and talked my husband into going out and picking up fast food for dinner. I was craving tacos and a milk shake—I knew I would have no problem getting those down. And my husband was more than happy to oblige and off he went.

When my husband returned, we quickly devoured our dinner. Afterwards, he hid the evidence, down the hallway in the trashcan of an abandoned room. Full and happy, I was getting tired—again—so he turned out the lights and I easily fell asleep.

My husband then retreated back to the hideaway bed he had been sleeping on in my room each night. Again, he cracked opened the book he was reading, clipped on his reading light, and read as he would do every night during my stay in the hospital—until he too was ready to retire for the evening.

Arrivederci

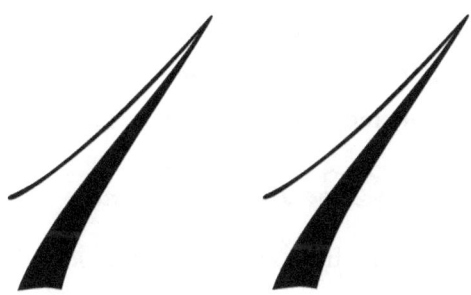

Unbelievable—I thought; my body was on some kind of weird clock. Again, I awoke in the middle of the night at exactly 11:00 p.m. Although—this time with the fan blowing—it was not my hot flashes that were bothering me; instead, it was my infections which were now stinging. I found myself whining and moaning all over again.

I called for the nurse, but this time a different nurse responded. I asked her for another Percocet to help with my pain. But she was insistent—I must stick to "doctor's orders" she told me. I could not have another Percocet until midnight. I explained that the stinging I was feeling was something new and my incisions were killing me.

As she turned on the lights, she could see that my incisions were very infected and oozing. The oozing had actually soaked through my hospital gown in several areas. In view of this, she did her best, as she tried to clean my wounds and gave me a new gown to put on. I wondered—just for a minute—if having the fan on might be making the germs throughout the hospital more airborne and as a result were further infecting my open wounds.

By the time we were done, it was 11:35 p.m. After what the two of us had just gone through together, I was sure she felt bad for me. She knew that I was not faking the pain and as a result she went ahead and gave me another Percocet—twenty-five minutes prematurely. Thank you God! I was exhausted again and able to fall back asleep.

Day 7 - Wednesday

Wednesday was finally here and I would be leaving Dr. X's hospital for good. My infections were beginning to overcome me and I realized I was very fragile. I prayed again for strength. And now dad was back—earlier than usual—as he knew I was scheduled to be transported by ambulance early that morning to Dr. TooCool's hospital.

My husband had the day off and had just kissed me goodbye. He went home to take a shower and freshen up before rejoining me. My mom, too, was taking the day off and would join us just before 9:00 a.m. when the paramedics were scheduled to arrive.

Preparations were in motion, my nurse kept administering injections—one after another—into my central line. I assumed they were medications and she was doing this to get me up to date with whatever I was on in preparation for my transport. I really didn't know what Dr. X's hospital was giving me—I had never asked. Thinking back to the conversation Dr. X and I had about electrolytes, maybe they were giving me magnesium, potassium, calcium, phosphate, and sodium. Maybe they were giving me various antibiotics to fight my ensuing infections . . . Again, I really didn't know.

She was back—for the seventh time—in less than two hours. I had been complaining to her that I was getting more and more nauseous. Consequently, she gave me a Protonix to ease the nausea before leaving again. Just what I needed I thought—NOT!

"Barfffffffffffffffffffffffffffffffffffff"

"Barffffffffffffffffffffffffffffffffffffffff"

Without any warning I began vomiting violently. I immediately grabbed one of my pillows from behind my head and held it hard against my abdomen as I was sure I was breaking my incisions open.

"Barffffffffffffffffffffffffffffffffffffff," right into my pillow.

"Barfffffffffffffffffffffffffffffffff," again, I feared I was breaking my sutures and hoping I was holding myself together with the pillow at the same time.

"Barfffffffffffffffffffffffffff," I couldn't stop.

"Barfffffffffffffffffffffffffffffffffffff"

"Barffffffffffffffffffffffffffffffffffffff"

Poor dad—I couldn't talk—I couldn't come up for enough air to speak to him. He did not know what to do—he looked panicked—he was in shock. In between vomiting episodes, I was trying to communicate to him—pointing to the nurse's call button so he could press it.

"Barffffffffffffffffffffffffffff"

"Barfffffffffffffffffffff"

As luck would have it, in the middle of my vomiting episode, flowers were being delivered. They were from my CPA against my wishes—okay—I'd given him a pass since he was not told "no flowers." And now, the delivery person was looking at me, asking where I would like the flowers.

"LADY, I DON'T CARE!"

76

No, I didn't say that to her, even though I felt like it. At last, realizing she was not going to get a response from me, she saw a shelf—above the bed my husband had been sleeping on—and placed the flowers on the shelf. Subsequently, she hurried out of my room.

Immediately behind her, three nurses came running in to attend to me. They didn't need the call button as they could hear me violently vomiting from down the hall. Finally, my vomiting episode had stopped and I was a mess. But I felt much better, now that I had gotten most of the stuff they were administering into my system out.

My poor dad was in shock and had silently left my room as soon as the nurses arrived. Later, I would learn that he had retreated to the lobby at the hospital entrance. Apparently, he was just sitting in a chair staring at a wall in some sort of trance when my husband arrived. I knew me being in the hospital was taking a toll on him and neither one of us had expected my violent vomiting episode on top of all the other drama.

My mother—for years—was a stay at home mom and she had always taken care of everything. It hadn't occurred to me that dad never took care of us when we were sick because mom was always there. He had been with me now because he was newly retired and had the time. Their roles had reversed and mom still had another few months to work before she would be of retirement age. And he probably had never experienced any of us kids sick and vomiting or even changed a diaper for that matter.

My husband had come through the lobby doors and immediately noticed my dad in the lobby just staring at a wall.

"What's wrong?" my husband asked my dad.

Deep in thought, my dad gave no response. He seemed catatonic staring straight ahead at the wall.

"Snap out of it!" my husband hollered as he thought something horrible had happened from the lack of response he was getting from my dad.

My dad then looked at my husband—his face white as a sheet, his eyes wide-eyed and gazed—and barely muttered, "It was horrible—she puked—all over the place."

My husband looked at my dad relieved and said, "Oh shit—that's all—I thought she had died or something."

My husband breathed a sigh of relief and then, together, they returned to my room.

Great, now the paramedics were there too. Typical of Dr. X's hospital, the only clean up the nurses gave me was the removal of my vomit soaked gown and a clean one to put on.

Can you believe it? My wounds were not even cleaned or attended to. No one had even looked to see if I had broken any sutures caused by my vomiting convulsions.

My mom had now arrived and she was speechless at the sight of me. She feared to say anything—as she didn't want to make matters worse. Right away my husband and dad took her outside my room to update her on what had happened. Meanwhile the cute ambulance guys prepared me for transport.

At this point, I didn't have any nourishment inside me at all—I was probably dehydrated from my recent vomiting episode—and I was so weak my arms were shaking. When I tried to sit up to move onto the gurney the paramedics had prepared, I was in a tremendous amount of pain—not to mention, scared out of my mind. I was about to undergo another surgery—too soon after my last two—and to make matters worse I was in an increasingly fragile state. Still, I knew I had to find the strength within me to get through this.

On top of everything else, I was angry. At least someone who was diagnosed with cancer—or some other fatal disease—had time to prepare and reflect. Me, I just opted for a "routine hysterectomy." I have had no time to prepare if I was to die; for instance, last great meal, last night on the town, and the likes. Reality was—if my infections didn't kill me—this third surgery could kill me. Then, I abruptly stopped myself; and thought, now I was just being morbid. Instead, I silently prayed.

Hospitals Pitted Against Hospitals

Lying in the ambulance, on the way to Dr. TooCool's hospital, I waved to my parents whom I could see directly behind the ambulance. My husband was behind them. The paramedic must have noticed my gesture. As he smiled, he told me that even though I could see them, they couldn't see me. I guess windows in ambulances are one-way.

During the ride, one paramedic sat in the back with me—monitoring my vitals—while the other drove. The inside of the ambulance reminded me of a military vehicle, very metal and stark. We made small talk and they told me they had orders to wait for me at Dr. TooCool's hospital so that they could transport me back to Dr. X's hospital. Again, I just smiled and stayed silent.

Finally, we arrived at Dr. TooCool's hospital. I was trembling and very weak. It would take all of my strength just to get in and out of the wheelchair and into my next hospital bed. More nurses—more hook ups.

Again, I felt like I was going to die. Then I paused and wondered for a moment, "Why was it that my thought process kept bringing me back to these same words?" Was this a subliminal message of what was to come?

Right away my thought was interrupted and I was startled. A priest from the Catholic church was at my bedside and wanted to pray with me. Yes, I was Christian, so I thought—although I didn't attend church on a regular basis. And yes, I was in a Catholic hospital. Nevertheless, this felt like last rites.

Knee jerk reaction, I asked my mom, "Please—make him go away?"

"Of course," she said looking into my pleading eyes.

Unbelievable, I was there for a CT scan scheduled for 10:00 a.m., which needed to precede my surgery at noon and now Dr. TooCool's hospital wanted to play paperwork beforehand. They asked the paramedics, who were still there in a waiting area, if Dr. X's hospital had sent my paperwork. The paramedics knew nothing about any paperwork, their orders were simple, transport me from Dr. X's hospital to Dr. TooCool's hospital and back.

So Dr. TooCool's hospital called Dr. X's hospital and asked if they could provide them with the necessary information. In order to properly register me, they needed to know things, such as: what had happened to me, why was I being seen, what medications I was on, what kind of insurance did I have, and so on. But Dr. X's hospital would not provide Dr. TooCool's hospital with any paperwork or information on me. They would only say that I was there for a procedure and thereafter I would be returning back to their care.

Getting nowhere, Dr. TooCool's hospital turned back to me and started asking me all kinds of paperwork questions—obviously we were starting from scratch. Still, I didn't have most of the answers. Before my hysterectomy, I was told not to bring anything with me, so I had left everything at home.

Then, I tried to facilitate, by explaining to my husband where all my insurance and hospital pre-admissions paperwork were at home. Yet, when I looked over at him, he seemed completely overwhelmed and I quickly told him not to worry. Instead, I asked him for my cell phone—he had it and handed it to me.

Next, I called human resources at my place of employment. Of course, there was no answer. I called another human resources gal—no answer. Finally, I frantically called a friend who worked with me there—thank you, Jesus! She answered. I was exhausted and could feel myself deteriorating. Thus, I handed the phone over to my mom to take over.

My mom worked with my friend over the phone and retrieved the insurance information I needed. She then passed the information on to Dr. TooCool's hospital. In addition, she told Dr. TooCool's hospital as much as she knew about my ordeal and what had happened, since Dr. X's hospital was not talking.

After an initial examination by Dr. TooCool's hospital—still holding me in admissions until all their paperwork was completed—they were further alarmed. The staff could see that I was in very bad shape and were shocked when they lifted my gown for the first time. Clearly my incisions were very infected, I smelt like vomit, I had blisters and bruising, I was still stapled, and I had JP drains hanging off the sides of my abdomen. I looked ghastly and the nurse immediately reported her findings to a supervisor at the admissions desk.

More alarms were going off for Dr. TooCool's hospital staff. As a result, they once again tried contacting Dr. X's hospital for any information on me, but again to no avail. This non-communication between hospitals would continue and become a reoccurring theme throughout my ordeal.

Thirty minutes had now gone by and I noticed that the paramedics were still hanging around. And so, I asked why? I thought after the paperwork debacle, the paramedics would have been informed that I would not be returning to Dr. X's hospital. After again confirming with the nursing staff that I would not be returning to Dr. X's hospital, I asked that the paramedics be told they could go. Immediately, they took care of it and the paramedics left.

I was so hungry and thirsty—I had nothing in my system. I was told no food or water twelve hours before surgery, which I had complied with. Even so, I had not anticipated my violent vomiting episode just before leaving Dr. X's hospital. As I attempted to explain this to a nurse, she insisted that if I had any food or water now, they would have to post-pone my surgery—so I suffered without.

It was finally 10:00 a.m. and the CT lab technicians were there to wheel me to the lab. Apparently, being on Heparin didn't interfere with being stuck with yet another needle—this time it was to inject contrast dye into my system before taking CT images. Moments later, the CT scan was done.

Afterwards, a nurse, who I will call nurse-Angel, appeared to wheel me to my next destination. Instead of taking me to the inpatient ward, she took me to their Progressive Care ward, which was a level of care in between the CCU and their inpatient ward. Coincidently, after my mother told the nurses about my nightmare at Dr. X's hospital, she asked that I be placed in a private room. Then, she was pleasantly surprised when they told her that based on my condition, I would be placed in their Progressive Care ward in which most of the rooms were private rooms.

Along the way, I noticed that this journey was a long one—not just hallways and corridors but in and out of elevators as well. Dr. TooCool's hospital was huge. As nurse-Angel was wheeling me into my new room, I stayed silent. I noticed that she was wheeling me into a private room—a corner room with a window. I observed it was daylight and could see that the trees were blowing in the wind.

There was a small desk and chair just to the left of the room. Cabinets and bookcases were mounted to the wall directly above and to the right of the desk. At the back of the room there were more chairs and a side table that was positioned next to where nurse-Angel had pushed my bed into place. On my left (right side of the room) I again had a private bathroom—the room felt cozy.

"Well—here you are—this is your room," she said energetically. "I work days and will be your primary nurse during the day shift Monday through Friday."

"Thank you," I said.

"I have written my name up on the whiteboard along with my schedule," she said, pointing to the whiteboard mounted on the wall next to the door.

"Day shift hours are 9:00 a.m. to 6:00 p.m.—but we usually hand off our patients at 5:00 p.m. and do our paperwork between 5:00 p.m. and 6:00 p.m. Each time you have a new nurse, they will do the same," she gasped, as she finally got my bed locked down.

"Thank you," I said.

"They placed you in our Progressive Care ward, which is usually reserved for heart patients," she continued. "However, in your case, I was told that you were in a serious state and would be staying in our unit."

I smiled.

"What happened to you?" she asked as she positioned a large metal platform connected to a long arm under the middle of my bed.

"What is that?" I asked.

"This is the scale we use to weigh patients when they are not supposed to be out of bed," she answered.

"Wow! I've never seen such a thing," I said.

"It's kind of cool," she added.

"It is," I said with a giggle as my bed was now moving.

"So what happened to you?" she asked again.

"Well—I went in for what was supposed to be a routine hysterectomy—but something went wrong," I answered. "My doctor closed me up—after thinking he had stopped the bleeding—and left the hospital. A couple of hours later my anesthesiologist, who was surprised to learn that I was in the CCU, came by to check on me. When he arrived, he found that I was internally bleeding, no blood had been ordered, and I was near death—my blood pressure was 80/20."

Nurse-Angel's eyes were as big as saucers as she was very much intrigued.

"Anyway, I guess by the end of it all, they had given me twelve-units of blood before they were done," I continued. "A new doctor came to my rescue and saved my life during the emergency surgery and stopped the bleeding."

"If he saved your life—why are you here?" she asked.

"Four days later—after they took me off my epidural—my pain level shot through the roof," I answered. "Apparently my iliac artery was sutured and now I need a third surgery to break the suture and potentially implant a femoro-femoral bypass graft to restore the blood flow to my leg."

Her face was filled with disbelief and shock.

"Not to worry—though—none of this happened in your hospital," I quickly added.

"Well—I'm glad you're still here," she said.

She then disappeared just for what seemed like a few seconds and then returned with another nurse, who I will call, nurse-Mother. Apparently, nurse-Mother had just read the notes in my admissions paperwork and she seemed alarmed with respect to my current condition.

"Hello—I am the head nurse here in this unit," she said. I've been reading through your admissions paperwork and I understand you are in very bad shape."

"Yes," I said.

"May I take a look at your incisions?" she asked.

"Yes," I replied, lifting my gown to expose my incisions.

"Your wounds are extremely infected," she said.

I nodded in agreement.

"Well—I can tell you—you are in the best possible place you can be right now," she informed me, as she seemed eager to get my ensuing infections under control.

"Great," I said.

"We have our own 'wound care' specialists and lab here at the hospital," she continued. "I am going to ask that one of the lab technicians come in—to take some cultures—so they can begin growing the bacteria from the infections. This will help us find an antibiotic to fight your infections."

"Thank you," I said.

86

"But before we begin, I am going to have nurse-Angel take some pictures of the current state of your wounds," she continued. "We need to document the condition you arrived in before moving forward."

"I'm fine with that," I reassured. "With everything I have been through I am not shy."

Moments later, nurse-Angel returned armed with a camera and soon lights were flashing. She took several pictures and documented the same.

"I have called the 'wound care' lab and they are sending a technician in," nurse-Angel confirmed.

"How long do you think it will take them to figure out what to give me to fight my infections?" I asked.

"No one knows for sure—sometimes it takes days for the cultures to react to an antibiotic," nurse-Angel continued. "In the meantime, we will be drawing your blood every few hours to monitor your white blood cell count. That way we will be able to determine if the infections are getting better or worse."

"Thank you," I said.

"Here is our standard issued pillow we give to everyone in our ward," she said, handing me a round yellow pillow with a large smiley face and bandage on the front.

"What is this?" I giggled, as I could not help myself from smiling back at the pillow.

"Well—like I said earlier—this ward is usually filled with heart patients and they too have upper body incisions," she answered. "So we give everyone a pillow—to hold hard against their upper body—anytime they have to cough. It will help prevent breaking open your incisions."

"This is great!" I said. "I love it."

"There's more," she said.

"What?" I asked, still smiling.

"Just before a patient is discharged, we try to get any of the nurses that had been attending to that particular patient to sign the pillow," she said. "Then the patient gets to take it home."

"You guys are awesome," I said. "Thank you!"

"You're very welcome," she said.

Dr. TooCool arrived.

"Hey there—I see that they already have you situated in your new room," he said.

"Yes, thank you," I replied.

"I've reviewed the CT images and it looks like your leg has further deteriorated since the last CT scan," he said. "At this point—even with breaking the suture—you will still have very little blood flow to your leg causing continued chronic pain and potential loss of your limb. So as I recommended before, I think we should proceed with the arterial femoro-femoral bypass graft. It will restore the blood flow to your leg giving you back the use of your leg."

"You're the boss," I said. "I trust you and I am fine with your decision—especially if is going to give me back the use of my leg and the pain will be gone too."

"Okay—great," he said as he pulled out a piece of paper and pen.

"As part of the procedure, I will be making two vertical incisions on either side of your groin," he explained.

"Okay," I said.

"The first incision will be lower and a little longer to enable me room to go in and cut the suture that is blocking your blood flow in that leg," he continued, drawing a picture of a torso with two legs. He then marked the area where he would be making the first vertical incision—approximating the location of the suture.

"Ah-huh," I said watching him.

"I've brought along the fem-fem vascular graft that I will be implanting in you," he continued, putting down the pen and paper and holding up a tube like device.

Weird looking I thought—it was about seven-inches long.

"It will be implanted in your groin area here," he said as he positioned the graft over my groin.

"And the second incision will be at the other end of the graft?" I asked, looking where he was holding the graft over my groin.

"That is correct," he answered.

"Here—let me go back to the drawing," he continued, putting the graft down and picking up the pen and paper again.

"Here is where the second incision will be," he said, finishing his drawing.

"So how long will the graft last?" I asked.

"The graft is temporary and will typically last ten years—but I have heard of them lasting more than twenty-five years," he answered.

"How will I know if it needs to be replaced?" I asked.

"You will know," he reassured.

"But—how?" I pressed.

"More than likely you'll be in extreme pain, and if that does happen, you would need to get to emergency right away," he answered.

"Is there some sort of follow-up program?" I asked.

"Yes—you will be placed under annual surveillance to monitor the longevity of your graft," he answered.

"Okay," I said. "And thank you so much for everything you are doing—I really do appreciate it."

"You're very welcome," he said. "Well—I am going to leave now to prep for surgery. I will see you then."

Great, more surgeries to look forward to down the road—I thought. But if my graft lasted me twenty-five years that meant I would only potentially need a couple of more surgeries. Later, I would research "femoro-femoral bypass grafts" in which I have provided my findings in Chapter 22. Then—and only then—I would learn that Dr. TooCool's numbers were way off. I would potentially need eight to ten more surgeries over my lifetime.

To make matters worse, if these reoccurring surgeries were considered pre-existing conditions, who was supposed to pay for them? Of course there's always private insurance available to an unsuspecting patient with no alternatives. But as luck would have it, I was fortunate. I had dual coverage (HMO and PPO) and would be okay as long as my current coverage didn't lapse.

No White Lights

13

Finally, I was headed to surgery—more hallways, corridors, and elevators. I still had not cried nor felt the need to cry—other than from pain. Again, I silently prayed to God—as this too was now becoming more and more routine now. Yet I was still confident that I would be okay once this surgery was over.

During surgery prep, they were hooking me up to an IV and other equipment—I would be given a spinal so I would not feel any pain during surgery. Soon I was introduced to the players who would assist: the anesthesiologist—who I will call Dr. Oblivious—the nurse, a data technician, and others. Lastly, Dr. TooCool arrived, making small talk before leaving to go "scrub up." Lights out for me.

This surgery also went too long—way too long—as a result, I actually woke up during the surgery; thank you God for the spinal!

Again my family was left in the dark, sitting in the waiting room wondering what was happening. But for me waking up in surgery, I would not have known what really had happened during my surgery. I was completely conscious when I woke up in surgery. I was not seeing "white lights" at the end of any tunnel—so I knew I couldn't be dead. Even so I pretended I had heard nothing and would ask to be put back to sleep.

Waking up in surgery was a very surreal moment in my life—and scary. I immediately heard voices and felt like I was freezing to death. I was shaking uncontrollably, but my chills seemed to be localized to the upper right side of my body. My left side was warm and covered with blankets, but on my right, my arm was exposed to the cold air of the OR causing my chills. Why was I awake I wondered?

As I listened, I heard Dr. TooCool and Dr. Oblivious bantering back and forth.

"Ha-ha—you are the one that always has to have the fanciest cars—fanciest toys," Dr. Oblivious teased.

"All right," interrupted Dr. TooCool.

"Even the fanciest surgical tools—you couldn't be satisfied with the standard surgical tools," Dr. Oblivious continued.

"Yes—yes—I know," said Dr. TooCool, frantically trying to stop Dr. Oblivious' taunting.

I was alarmed that I was awake. And from the tone of the conversation—going back and forth between the two—I could tell something was wrong, but I felt like I was freezing to death. I had to do something, so I gently and slowly started raising my exposed arm up in the air and back down—over and over again—to get someone's attention.

Amazingly, I had done this several times and still no one was paying any attention to me. From their continued tone, I could tell Dr. TooCool was uptight. Hence, I decided to stop raising my arm and lied there motionless—quietly listening. I didn't want to further startle Dr. TooCool and possibly make things worse.

"If you were using standard surgical tools—the tool may not have broken off—and you wouldn't be wasting time trying to retrieve it," Dr. Oblivious continued, not about to stop taunting.

"I have another surgery scheduled and I'm running late," Dr. TooCool said abruptly. "I need to find an available surgeon."

Dr. Oblivious was quiet now.

Next, I heard Dr. TooCool on his cell phone—while he was still operating on me.

"I'm still in surgery—I need to find someone to take over my next surgery that is scheduled in an hour," Dr. TooCool said.

"No—this surgery is taking longer than I expected," he said.

"What about Dr. Old?" he asked. "Is he available?"

I was shocked. How sanitary was this, Dr. TooCool on his cell phone—having a conversation with someone while he was still operating on me?

And more importantly, why the hell was I awake? Why hadn't anyone noticed that I was awake? I was sliced open, lying on an operating table, and awake during my own surgery. Thank you God— again—for the spinal, as I was sure I would be in extreme pain without it. I have since researched "spinal, epidural, and general anesthesia" and have provided my findings herein.[17]

Still freezing, I nevertheless, laid there frozen and endured my chills. I feared that Dr. TooCool was in over his head—again, I didn't want to alarm him and make things worse. Instead, I decided to take in the moment and looked around the room. I had never seen an Operating Room before—I thought.

As I looked around the room, I could see the bright lamp above me and it was blinding. But I couldn't see Dr. TooCool. They had blankets piled high on my chest obscuring my view; however, I could hear him in front of me—operating away I assumed. The room seemed cold, very stark, and uninviting— I thought. I could still hear Dr. Oblivious, on my left, chatting at Dr. TooCool. And I knew there was at least one other person in the room, behind me on a computer tapping away. Finally, I heard excitement in the room.

"I got it! I got it!" Dr. TooCool exclaimed.

Thank you God! Apparently—from what I heard of their conversation—after successfully cutting away the suture, the tip of Dr. TooCool's surgical tool broke off and traveled down my leg. (This would become a cover up that still continues to this day.) As a result, Dr. ToolCool had spent nearly the entire surgery time trying to retrieve the broken off tool piece.

I waited another few seconds, as I still didn't want to startle Dr. TooCool. I didn't want to take the risk of him re-dropping the broken tool piece in my leg if that indeed was what he had retrieved. Silently I counted to ten. Then, once again, I slowly raised my right arm into the air one more time and spoke.

"Doctor?" I called out softly.

I could sense they were all startled as the room went silent.

"Yeees?" Dr. Oblivious replied obviously startled.

"I am cold," I said.

Still the room remained eerily silent as I spoke—you could have heard a pin drop.

"Get that heater over to her!" Dr. Oblivious quickly barked. "Re-wrap those blankets!"

"Thank you," I said softly. "Can you please put me back to sleep now?"

And the next thing I knew I was out like a light.

Lies and Near Overdose

A quick recap, my leg surgery was scheduled for 12:00 noon at Dr. TooCool's hospital. Surgery was supposed to last less than two hours, but instead lasted more than six hours. Although, Dr. TooCool was successful in breaking the suture that was around my iliac artery, he did not have time to implant my bypass graft. Instead, he spent the majority of the surgery time, retrieving a piece of surgical tool that had broken off when he cut through the suture. After waking up during surgery— and listening to what had happened—I asked Dr. Oblivious to put me back to sleep. Following surgery I was moved to Post-Op at around 7:00 p.m. While I was in Post-Op, Dr. TooCool updated my husband and parents.

"Good evening," Dr. TooCool said.

"Good evening," my husband said.

"Hi," said dad and mom in unison.

"First, let me tell you that her exploratory surgery was partially successful—I was able to break the suture that was tied around her iliac artery," Dr. TooCool said.

Are you kidding me? What exploratory surgery? This surgery was to break the suture and then implant the fem-fem bypass graft. Hadn't just before surgery, Dr. TooCool himself said that removing the suture would not be enough to restore my blood flow. Hence, he would be doing both procedures—breaking the suture and implanting the bypass graft.

"However, during her surgery, a blood clot broke off in her leg and I spent the majority of the time retrieving the blood clot," he continued.

This was crazy! Earlier I'd been told that the blood clots were arterial and couldn't do any damage. I had also been told that the blood clots were lodged in such an area in my leg, where they could not remove nor be reached to remove.

"She will still have to undergo another surgery to implant the femoro-femoral bypass graft," he said. "However, I believe in her current state it would be dangerous, she's been through too much. So I would like to post-pone the next surgery for several months."

"Oh my God," my mother cried.

"What are you saying?" my husband asked. "How is she supposed to go home if she has no use of her left leg?"

"And what about all the pain her leg is causing her?" my dad interjected.

"We can give her medication for the pain," Dr. TooCool said. "In the meantime, I want to put her on Coumadin—a blood thinner regimen—until she is ready for surgery. The thinning of her blood should also help with her pain."

"Doctor, isn't Coumadin a dangerous drug?" my dad asked. "I thought with the slightest cut she could unknowingly bleed to death."

"Yes—but without the blood thinner, coupled with not having the use of her leg, her condition will worsen. She'd be in constant pain."

My husband and parents bought his story.

Finally, my husband and parents were allowed to see me—one at a time—in Post-Op. I was in and out of consciousness. Later, I was told that once again I was acting like a violent animal—angry and distraught. When I was awake I would ask questions like, "What day is it?" "What time is it?" It was like I had no idea where I was or what I was doing—I was completely disoriented. And it seemed as though I was deteriorating for the worse.

Then my husband had an "Ah-ha!" moment. He remembered that I had, had a similar reaction at Dr. X's hospital, when they were giving me Ativan in the CCU there. He also flashed back to when he saw the same reaction from his father, several months earlier, after brain surgery—he too had been given Ativan.

My husband immediately pulled my mother aside and told her that they had me on Ativan again. Together, they talked to the nurse in charge of Post-Op and demanded that I be taken off Ativan. My husband explained that I was having an adverse reaction to the Ativan and he had seen it before at Dr. X's hospital when I was in Post-Op there. They complied and took me off the Ativan.

When I did become conscious, I was completely out of it and could barely keep my eyes open. In fact, each time I tried to wake up, I felt like my eyes were rolling back into my head. Then, I was only awake for a couple of—what felt like—seconds before passing out again.

Again, I struggled to wake up. I was so thirsty and my lips felt chapped—I was dehydrated. When I begged for water, I was told "no," but that I could have ice-chips at 10:00 p.m. Instinctively, I looked up at the clock and saw that it was 8:00 p.m.— then I passed out.

Yet again, I struggled to wake up and looked to the clock, but it was only 9:00 p.m. I looked at the nurse and I nodded "yes" and passed out again—I knew the drill.

This was—by far—the hardest time I had trying to wake up after surgery. When I had asked to be put back to sleep, I remember being knocked out pretty much instantly. But now I began to question if Dr. Oblivious might have overdosed me. Waking up felt impossible—I kept literally passing out seconds after coming to.

Finally, I woke again just minutes before 10:00 p.m. Odd, my body seemed to be on some kind of subconscious time clock again. I looked to the nurse once more and this time she nodded "yes." I was finally awake and given ice-chips in which I savored every bite. I felt relieved, but on the other hand I was angry—I knew I was going to have to endure a fourth surgery.

About a half hour later, a couple of orderlies arrived and wheeled me back to my room in the Progressive Care ward. Nurse-Angel had gone off shift and now I had a new nurse, who I will call, nurse-Nightwatch. She too, was very warm-hearted and had written her information on the whiteboard.

"Hi there," she said with a smile.

"Hi," I groaned, still groggy and in a much weakened state.

"What happened?" she asked, as she positioned the oxygen tubes around my neck and inserted the prongs into my nostrils. "We had expected you back in your room around 4:00 p.m. and we were concerned."

Now it was nearly 11:00 p.m.

"Sorry—I'd rather not talk about it right now," I said. "I'm angry— I woke up in surgery and now I have to have yet another surgery."

She was baffled.

"Can you do me a favor?" I asked. "My family is somewhere in the hospital and I am sure they are looking for me. Could you please find them and show them to my room?"

She nodded and went on her way.

Moments later, my husband and parents arrived. As I watched them walk in, I decided in my mind that they already knew what had happened—not knowing that Dr. TooCool had told them a completely different story from what really had happened. They looked tired and distraught. Their heads were down as if they didn't know how to break the news that I would require a fourth surgery.

So I decided to save them the chore and blurted out angrily, "I already know the surgery wasn't successful and that I have to have a fourth surgery."

My husband and parents were silent. Although they looked relieved that they didn't have to break the news to me, they also looked lifeless—they too were suffering. Then it happened, I finally broke down in tears—I was crying—and this time it was not related to pain. I did not know how much more I could take. I had reached my breaking point when I realized I was going to have yet a fourth surgery.

So I asked my husband to stay the night with me. He agreed and then walked my parents to their car, telling them he would see them the next day. It was 11:30 p.m. and we were all exhausted—so I kept silent. Meanwhile, nurse-Nightwatch took care of getting a roll out bed set up under the window for my husband to sleep on.

Before going to bed, nurse-Nightwatch arranged for me to have a hospital phone at my bedside—instead of me using my cell phone. I guess cell phones are frowned upon in hospitals—does something to their equipment. Soon after, I moved the phone into my bed with me for convenience.

I was exhausted and still very groggy. I was obviously still fighting the affects from all the drugs they had given me—during and after surgery. Finally, I could no longer keep my eyes open, and once again, I fell into a deep sleep.

Cover Up

I woke up from what I thought had been a full night's sleep and I was starving. Thinking I had over slept, I was mad because I thought I had missed breakfast. I hadn't eaten since dinner Tuesday night. Then I looked over and saw that my husband was still there. He was lying on the roll out bed.

"Honey—wake up," I said.

"Huh—what—what?" he said, obviously half asleep.

"It's morning, you're late for work," I said.

"Huh?" he said, looking at his watch. "It is 1:00 a.m. in the morning; you've only been sleeping for a little over an hour."

"I'm sorry," I said.

"No worries sweetie—go back to sleep," he said in his usual kindhearted tone of voice.

Again I felt disoriented. It was as if my internal clock from Post-Op was continuing to wake me every hour on the hour. However, now it wasn't ice-chips that I craved, it was food. Then, with the answers from my husband and realizing I had only slept about an hour, I fell back into a deeper sleep this time.

Day 8 - Thursday

Although usually an early riser, this morning was different. I was awakened by a phone call just before 6:00 a.m. It was Dr. X and I was mystified.

"Good morning—I hope I didn't wake you," he said.

"I'm up," I said angrily.

"Drs. Lifesaver and TooCool and I, spent several hours on a conference call late last night that ran into the early morning hours," he said. "We discussed your surgery and how to move forward."

I was still very angry and didn't want to hear it. I reflexively interrupted him and said, "I know what happened! I woke up in surgery! And I don't want to talk about it right now!"

Then I hung up on him just as abruptly as he had awakened me. Afterwards, I was stunned at what I had done. After all, it would have been interesting to hear what he had to say—I thought. Oh well, too late—I thought again. I was exhausted and was able to fall back to sleep.

Around 7:00 a.m., I was awake again and nurse-Nightwatch had just come into my room.

"Hey—I'm getting off shift soon," she whispered.

"Uh-huh," I said, as she seemed very mysterious.

I then looked around my room. My husband was gone—he must had left for work already, I thought.

She then leaned closer and whispered, "I checked your chart—even though it does not state that you actually woke up in surgery—there is clearly a notation where Dr. Oblivious administers you a second dose of a different kind of anesthesia."

She was now shaking her head, "yes." In her mind this proved that I had indeed awakened during surgery. That was the only logical explanation for the second dose of anesthesia by Dr. Oblivious.

I smiled and said, "Thank you."

"Oh—and another thing," she said.

"Yes?"

"I went ahead and pre-ordered you breakfast," she said. "I hope you like it. It will be here at 9:00 a.m."

"Thank you!" I cheered. "I love you! Thank you!"

Right on schedule, at 9:00 a.m., my dad showed up. Mom was at work. Although Dr. TooCool had briefed him last night, he still didn't know I had awoken during surgery.

"Dad—shut the door," I whispered.

Dad shut the door.

"I woke up during the surgery yesterday," I whispered.

My dad was in disbelief of what he was hearing.

"Nurse-Nightwatch pretty much confirmed it for me this morning," I continued.

Dad was silent.

"Knock—knock," we heard as the door started to open.

Now I was silent too.

"I have your breakfast here," said a staff member, taking a tray from her cart and setting it on my side table next to my bed.

"Oh—thank you," I said.

104

"I'm going to leave you a menu order form and pencil so you can circle what you'd like for lunch and dinner," she instructed. "I'll be back in an hour to pick it up. Each day you will be given the same—like this one—to fill out for the next day. And it is usually picked up the following hour."

"Thank you," I said.

This was cool—it reminded me of the cruise ships we traveled on. Every evening a breakfast menu would be left in our stateroom, for us to fill out and hang on the outside of our doorknob. This gave us the option of having breakfast delivered to our cabin or going down to the dining room for breakfast.

"Here," I said, handing the menu and pencil to my dad. "Go ahead and fill it out—mark down anything you want to try as well. I can't concentrate right now."

"So—you woke up during surgery?" my dad asked.

"Yes," I whispered. "But I don't want to talk about it right now—I don't want anyone to hear us. I just want to play nice so that I can get better and get out of here."

After removing the oxygen tubes from my nose, I sat up and shared my breakfast with my dad. This was the first time I had been served food in Dr. TooCool's hospital and the food was really good—coffee, eggs, bacon, fruit, juice, toast, and butter. Apparently my husband and parents had discovered the cafeteria the day before. Later they would tell me that it was a large cafeteria, reasonably priced, and it even had a salad bar and yogurt machine.

Shortly after breakfast, nurse-Mother interrupted us—my second encounter with her and dad's first.

"Hi—I am the head nurse here in the Progressive Care ward," she said, introducing herself to my dad, extending her hand out politely.

"Hi," my dad replied, shaking her hand.

"I would like to look at your wounds again," she said, looking at me now.

"Okay," I said. "Dad, do you want to leave until after the examination is over?"

"Yep," he said, jumping to his feet—he knew the drill.

"I am still very concerned about your wounds," she said as she closed my door and then raised my gown. "They still appear to be getting worse and many of the infected areas are oozing with puss."

Nurse-Angel walked in and nurse-Mother turned to her.

"You will need to clean her wounds with saline and redress them in gauze—twice a day," she instructed.

"Yes—of course. I will get the supplies and do it now," she said efficiently and then exited the room.

Interesting, this was in complete contradiction to what Dr. X had instructed at his hospital. He had wanted my incisions left exposed. Could this be what had caused my ensuing infections?

"I am going to order more lab cultures to be taken," she said. "The previous cultures have not responded to anything. And we are very concerned with your white blood cell count. It is very high—over 20—indicating severe infections."

"I understand," I said.

"We're further concerned that you still have blood in your urine—see the red-brown coloration," she said, holding up my catheter bag.

"I understand," I said.

"Get some rest, and I'll see you later," she said.

They all seemed truly concerned for my well-being. Later I would research "white blood cell count vs. red blood cell count" and include my findings herein.[18]

106

After nurse-Angel returned with the supplies to clean my oozing wounds, I stopped her. I told her that I was in a lot of pain and was afraid that cleaning my wounds would make the pain worse. So she quickly stepped out of my room again to consult nurse-Mother. She returned with a Darvocet—another pain medication—in which I took.

Twenty minutes later, the Darvocet kicked in and nurse-Angle cleaned and dressed my wounds. She then gave me a sponge bath and helped me into a fresh gown. When I was done, she gave me a toothbrush and a small bowl to spit into so I could brush my teeth from my bed.

Still, I continued to suffer from hot flashes. I told nurse-Angel that Dr. X's hospital had given me a fan to help with my hot flashes, and asked if this hospital had any fans. She explained that fans were not allowed because they stir up air and blow airborne germs around. Well, that made sense—I had actually had that thought cross my mind at Dr. X's hospital when the fan there was blowing on me.

Shortly after our conversation, dad walked in and quietly told me that he called my mom to update her on my morning news. With all the mishaps, I was beginning to feel completely defeated and overwhelmed. Even so, I wanted to play nice, in the hope that someone would fix me. I wanted the use of my left leg again. I wanted my infections healed. I wanted the pain to go away. I wanted to go home.

I was nauseous again, so I called nurse-Angel to my room to complain about my nausea. I told her that I thought the Darvocet was upsetting my stomach. I asked if I could be placed back on Percocet instead, like I had been at Dr. X's hospital. She checked with the doctors, and once again I was given Protonix to help with my nausea, and Percocet to help with my pain.

Later that morning, Dr. TooCool arrived.

"Good morning," he said.

"Good morning," I replied.

"How are you feeling today?" he asked.

"I've been better," I replied.

"Yes—I can see that your white blood cell count is very high because of your infections," he said as he flipped through my chart.

"So I would like to put off your next surgery—to implant the arterial femoro-to-femoral bypass graft—for at least three months until you are stronger."

This was the first time that I had heard surgery would be postponed.

"In the meantime—as I mentioned before—I want to put you on Coumadin, a strong blood thinner" he continued. "Once your infections are under control, I can prescribe Coumadin in a pill form that you can take from home until you return for your next surgery."

During our conversation, there was no mention of me waking up in surgery—or what had happened during my surgery—or what my husband and parents had been told.

I lost it! I broke down in tears, pleading with Dr. TooCool, "That was not the deal! I have my sons to bring up and I need the function of both my legs."

He quickly calmed me down and reluctantly said, "Okay—okay—I will do your next surgery sooner. But I can't do the surgery until your infections are under control. Your white blood cell count is still very high. I will check back with you tomorrow."

"Thank you!" I cried. "Thank you!"

"In the meantime—I will write the orders to put you on a Coumadin regimen now," he said.

"Okay," I said, still sniffling.

Shortly thereafter, nurse-Angel came in and gave me my first dose of Coumadin. I was scared. I knew Coumadin to be a much stronger blood thinner than what I had previously been on—Heparin. With the slightest scratch—I thought—I could bleed out. Throughout the day those thoughts would haunt me, creating periodic spells of anxiety. My dad, still there and listening, too, was also concerned. Later I would research "Heparin and Coumadin" and provide my findings herein.[19/20]

Late that afternoon, Dr. Lifesaver came by to check on me. After his initial examination, he removed all but one of my staples. Although I was apprehensive at first, the pain had no comparison to what I had already been through. As he began, he told me to take a deep breath and then when I exhaled he pulled out a staple. We went through this process approximately seventeen times—until all but one of the staples was removed. For now, he wanted to leave the one staple at the "T" where the two incisions intersected.

I told him that I was still in a lot of pain, constant and severe pain deep down in my pelvic area. He could plainly see that there was still blood in my urine in my catheter bag hanging at the foot of my bed. Still, he assumed most of my pain was being caused by the severity of my infections. So he asked nurse-Angel to come back to my room and clean and redress my incisions. After that, he left, telling me he would be back in a few days to check my status.

While nurse-Angel was cleaning my incisions, I was completely exposed, and my door was closed. Then—without even a knock—a Catholic priest barged in. He was the same priest who I will now call Priest Pester, who had freaked me out days earlier. I was horrified and told nurse-Angel to get him out of there. He was clueless and didn't want to take "no" for an answer. So I screamed, "GET OUT OF HERE!"

Finally, nurse-Angel was able to get rid of him. Afterwards, I told her that I wanted it stated in my chart that under no circumstance was he or any other priest allowed in my room. She completely understood where I was coming from and had no problem accommodating my wishes.

Dinner arrived as my family members were shuffling in and out. My oldest son was there, too, and hung out with my husband in the background. My parents had discovered the hospital's frozen yogurt and offered me some. It was delicious and refreshing, I immediately asked my dad if he could go and get me my own.

Now their conversation had turned back to me. I guess I had flipped over my round yellow pillow—after holding it to my stomach while I coughed—and they noticed the smiley face on it. They, too, thought it was adorable. My husband immediately named the pillow "Wilson." He said it reminded him of the movie Castaway with Tom Hanks. In the movie Tom Hanks is stranded on a desert island. He finds a volleyball on the beach and draws a smiley face on it (calling it Wilson), and proceeds to interact with it throughout the course of the film—it becomes his only companion.

My anxiety about being on Coumadin and the possibility of bleeding to death began to consume me. In an effort to try to calm myself down, I told my family I was tired and they quickly agreed to leave and return the next day. My husband, of course, would stay and again spend the night with me as he would do every night until I was discharged—with the exception of one night when my mom relieved him to give him a break. He had finished reading the last Harry Potter and was now on his second novel by David Morrell.

As well, they were taking blood from me every couple of hours. I had already had a run in with one lab technician, who wanted to draw blood from my arm earlier in the day. I stopped her and insisted that she do so through my central line. We argued, so I told her to get nurse-

Angel. She did and nurse-Angel drew my blood from my central line on behalf of the lab technician.

Consequently, I had a sleepless night, repeating the same argument many hours later with yet another lab technician. This lab technician had come in the middle of the night to draw my blood. I gasped. Had I not been awake to stop her, had she stuck my arm with a needle as I slept, I could possibly have bled to death. I thought that my fears might have been a bit exaggerated but they were my fears.

Day 9 - Friday

At approximately 6:00 a.m. I received an unannounced visit from Dr. X. He—again—was in his jogging clothes. He did not have "hospital privileges" at Dr. TooCool's hospital but he was here now.

"Good morning," he whispered.

"H—H— Hi," I said, surprised at the sight of him.

"So how are you doing?" he asked quietly.

"Not sure—you can ask the nurse to show you my chart," I answered.

"No—no—I am not supposed to be here," he said. "So they can't give me any information on you."

Apparently he had just snuck into my room. I wondered, had he come here out of concern for himself or me?

"My white count is still very high. I think it is over twenty and they are very concerned," I said.

Then—without another word—he slowly crept out of my room and magically disappeared. I wondered why the nursing staff didn't say anything to him or how he had gotten by them in the first place. I assumed that this was just typical of how doctors interacted with patients when they didn't have "hospital privileges" at a patient referred hospital.

Well, I guess he got what he wanted. Odd as it was, he would perform this same routine several more times before I would be discharged. Not sure why I had never asked Dr. TooCool's hospital whether or not his behavior was customary. Nor was I sure why I was always so forthcoming with updates for him—given how I felt about him and his hospital.

Right on schedule—at 9:00 a.m.—dad was back, but this time he had a gift for me. He knew I didn't want flowers, so he had brought me a scarf knitting kit, which he had bought from the hospital gift shop—he knew I was an avid knitter. I loved it and was immediately intrigued. Instead of yarn, it was a series of threads and ribbons combined to form a yarn-like string. The needles too were different, about one-third of an inch thick, but still the standard length. I happily thanked him.

Over breakfast, we discussed the anxiety the Coumadin was causing me. I updated him on the events of the day before, when a lab technician had tried to stick me with a needle to draw my blood; and a repeat performance last night with yet another technician. I told him that I feared someone was actually going to stick me with a needle while I slept. He didn't like the situation either.

Meanwhile, not one to keep a secret, my dad shared with me that my mom had forced her early retirement. She wasn't comfortable going to work every day—and leaving me—while I was still in the hospital. She too could foresee that I had a long recovery ahead of me and she wanted to help as much as she could. Friday would be her last day.

I was excited to hear the news and so was he. He retired a year earlier and was getting very bored. He and mom had been married for nearly fifty years and neither of them really knew what to do without the other. They enjoyed each other's company, and my siblings and I were very happy that our parents were still happily married after all these years.

My dad also told me that my middle brother and his significant other—whom had spent the last year out of state had accelerated their plans to return. They would be driving across country with their pets, returning home in the next day or so. They too were truly concerned about my health and felt the need to be close to me.

As promised, Dr. TooCool was back to check on me. My dad and I discussed our concerns with him about me being on Coumadin. We updated him on the incidents of the day before and the following night. He acknowledged our concerns and suggested that we do another CT scan on my leg to see if there had been any improvement since the surgery. I agreed and he scheduled the procedure for early that afternoon.

In the meantime, Dr. TooCool still wanted me to remain on Coumadin, so we reluctantly agreed. He reiterated that my white blood cell count was still over twenty—so surgery was still not an option. He would follow up again on Tuesday.

Once again I would prep for yet another CT scan—no food or water after 10:00 a.m. Subsequently, at around 3:00 p.m., a young lab tech came in and introduced himself. He told me he was ready to take me to the lab for my scan—so off I went.

When we arrived at the lab, he assisted me onto the bed of the CT machine and began prepping me for the scan. As he prepared the back

114

of my hand, I realized he was doing so to inject contrast dye using a needle! I screeched!

"Please—don't stick that needle in me!" I pleaded. "I'm on Coumadin and I can't be stuck with any needles. If you do—I could bleed to death."

"But we have "doctor's orders"—that your doctor signed and he wants us to inject the contrast dye before starting the scan," he explained.

"No—please call Dr. TooCool or nurse-Angel," I begged, not giving up.

He reluctantly retreated and called to confirm. Sure enough he was told to do the CT scan without using contrast dye. It was understood that without contrast dye the pictures would not be as clear. As a result, they performed the procedure without the dye.

By the time I got back to my room I was a wreck and full of anxiety. What else could possibly happen to me? If not for the seriousness of my situation this dark comedy of errors might have been humorous.

Right away I told my dad what had happened and it made him mad, too. He immediately went to the nurses' station and had a heart-to-heart with them. Afterwards, nurse-Angel must have gotten a hold of Dr. TooCool, because now they had new "doctor's orders" to stop administering Coumadin to me. And so, they did to my great relief.

Singing Bear Telegram

The weekend was almost here and the on-call doctors would be in and out doing their rounds. I had been in hospitals for nine days now. My infections were continuing to get worse. My white blood cell counts hit twenty-two, which was alarmingly high. Now, even the Percocet was not keeping the pain away.

In addition to doctors, nurse-Angel and nurse-Mother were now attending to me constantly. So far, the lab cultures had been resistant to the antibiotics the lab specialists were trying in an effort to fight my ensuing infections—I was in bad shape. Still, being the positive person I had always been, I was not giving up. I knew I'd get better and I would consider nothing less—so I continued to push myself.

As part of my personal course of therapy to regain my strength, I followed the hospital menu plan and ate nutritious meals as I knew the hospital was recording everything I ate. Additionally, I would use the back of my bed to exercise—doing mini pull-up reps—several times a day. As well, I made sure after each meal, I spent some time up and out of bed—sitting in a chair or walking around my room. I was still too weak to walk the halls outside my room. I also continued to do my breathing exercises—several times a day—using the AirLife Volumetric Incentive Spirometer they had given me. Later, I would research this device and I've provided my findings herein.[21]

Regardless of my positive mindset—considering what I had been through—the nursing staff felt the need to lift my spirits. Late that afternoon, around 4:00 p.m., I was alone when nurse-Angel and a couple of other nurses appeared at my door.

They had brought me a get-well card and a three-foot tall singing teddy bear. Her name was Dusty Rose and she was pink, with dark brown eyes, and wore a purple ribbon sash around her waist. She was accessorized with pearls and a white hat with a large rose in it. She was adorable. If you squeezed her paw, she would sing a song: LOVE by Milt Gabler and Bert Kaempfert. Inside the card, nurses-Angel, Nightwatch, Mother, and one other nurse had signed it.

"H—ee—yyy—how are you," the group sung.

"H—hi—what's this?" I asked, laughing and glassy eyed—touched by their kindness.

"Well—since you are so sweet, have been such a good patient, and have been in the hospital so long, we thought we'd bring you a little something to cheer you up," nurse-Angel replied, squeezing Dusty Rose's paw.

L is for the way you look at me
O is for the only one I see
V is very, very extraordinary

117

E is even more than anyone that you adore and

Love is all that I can give to you
Love is more than just a game for two
Two in love can make it
Take my heart and please don't break it
Love was made for me and you

"Thank you so much—you shouldn't have," I said, surprised by their gesture.

"We are all very concerned that we still have not found an antibiotic to fight your infections," nurse-Mother replied as she too had now joined the group. "And we know something went wrong—here at our hospital—causing you to require another surgery. So we wanted to do something for you."

"Yes—so the four of us got together and pooled our money so we could do something to cheer you up," nurse-Angel interrupted excitedly.

"Thank you again—you gals are great," I cheered.

The group then dispersed back to their patients and duties except for nurse-Angel.

Still in disbelief, I probed further and asked: "You must have lots of patients—why me—why would you pool your money together for a gift for me?"

"Well—we've really gotten attached to you," she answered. "Typically, in our ward, most of our patients are elderly. We are not accustomed to caring for someone so young. You remind us of ourselves. Besides, it wasn't that much, total cost was $68 split among the group of us."

"Well—thank you so much," I said.

Although, extremely grateful, their gesture spooked me. I didn't understand why they would be spending their hard earned money on a stranger. Then I looked up and noticed nurse-Angel still standing there—staring at my bewildered face.

"We are worried about you," she said. "You have been through so much and our wound care specialists have so far been unsuccessful. Your white count continues to rise and time feels like it is running out."

"What do you think my chances are—with the race against the clock—with respect to my infections?" I asked.

"I am not supposed to say anything, but nurse-Mother has informed us that things are looking grave if an antibiotic for your infections is not found soon," she whispered.

"But—they're still working on the lab cultures aren't they?" I asked.

"Yes—of course they are," she answered. "And you are very lucky that our hospital specializes in wound care—so you couldn't be in a better place under your circumstances."

"Well—I am confident that they will find an antibiotic and I will get better," I reassured her with a wink.

Okay, so time was running out, my white count was rising and my infections had still not stabilized. I rationalized that it had never crossed my mind throughout this whole ordeal that I could die. I believed in God. If He really wanted me—He surely would have taken me by now. God knows He's had plenty of opportunities to do so.

I was convinced that I was still here because I trusted God, I had a good heart, I had integrity, and I had a legacy to build. One that I dreamed would support not just our family, but thousands of future employees and their families too.

Although at this point, under the circumstances, I had to admit things were beginning to look very grim. Still, I knew I was in good hands. My nurses were attending to me around the clock, cleaning and caring for my infected wounds, and bathing me daily. And I was doing my part as well—eating, exercising, and getting up and around when I could. Whatever could be done was being done.

It was early evening now and my husband and parents were there; my husband looked exhausted. It was Friday night and my mom was officially retired. She wanted to spend some quality time with her daughter. So she turned to her favorite son-in-law and offered to spend the night with me—giving him a much needed break. (Yes, I am her only daughter, so he is her only son-in-law—hence, favorite.)

After hearing her offer, my husband's ears perked up as did mine. I was looking forward to a "girl's night"—and this was an offer my husband couldn't refuse. My mom would spend the night with me and he would go and hang out with his friends. He was thrilled. Not to mention, most of our friends knew very little—if anything—of what was going on. Now he would be able to decompress over drinks and tell our friends all of our war stories.

Shortly thereafter, my husband and dad said their goodbyes, and mom and I had our "girl's night" at the hospital in the Progressive Care ward. We started with dinner, followed by frozen yogurts, and reminisced about old times. I felt relaxed, like a ton of bricks had been lifted from my shoulders—now that I was no longer on Coumadin. I would actually be able to sleep tonight.

Colleagues

Living in the hospital was taking a toll on me. It had been ten days now and I was beginning to wonder if I'd ever see the light at the end of the tunnel and get discharged. I was bored out of my mind and I wanted to be productive. I wanted to catch up on television shows, read, or work on my company—something. Yet strangely my brain would not let me focus on such activities.

Instead, I listened to what my body was telling me, and spent my time resting and sleeping with the occasional out of bed, exercising, and socializing with friends and family. Not even coffee appealed to me. Instinctively, my body seemed to only want to do what was good for it—so I paid attention and complied.

Day 10 - Saturday

It was early Saturday morning. Mom and I, both early risers, had already had our coffee. She had slipped away to the cafeteria around 7:30 a.m. and surprised me with coffee before retreating home to my dad. I had not told her that I wasn't craving coffee. Consequently, I indulged in a few sips anyway to appease her. Girl's night was officially over and mom left.

My phone was ringing—the hospital phone I kept alongside me in bed. This time it was my youngest brother who was also living out of state. He was concerned about me and offered to fly in. I told him that would not be necessary. I explained that if he came now, I feared it would send a subliminal message to my mind that I was dying. I told him I didn't want to see him until I was well enough to actually enjoy our visit. He thought it sounded nuts—but knowing a little about how his sister thought, he understood.

As CEO of his own software company, we talked about the fashion and luxury goods company my husband and I were about to launch. (His company would be handling the e-commerce and web development for our businesses.) We discussed our online boutique and website as well as various timing and scheduling activities.

Then, as we were talking, I heard a click—someone was trying to get through. I told my brother someone was calling on the other line and I needed to pick up the call in case it was my husband. And so, we said our goodbyes and he told me he would call again soon.

I answered the other line. Well, I was wrong—it wasn't my husband—it was Dr. X. If he wasn't sneaking in—in the early morning hours—he was calling to check in. Not sure why, he never had anything to tell me and only wanted to pull information from me about my current condition. At least these visits or phone calls were always very short. Then just as I hung up my husband walked in!

The rest of the morning—between naps—my husband and I caught up on all the stories from our separate evening the night before. When I napped, he would spend his time reading or watching television. Things were very boring at the hospital it seemed.

Later that morning, we were greeted by one of Dr. Lifesaver's colleagues who I will call Dr. Feelgood. She was a very attractive tall slender woman with blonde hair—my husband immediately took notice. She had a grace about her and she seemed very caring. Apparently, she and Dr. Lifesaver shared a medical practice.

"Good morning," she said warmly.

"Good morning," I replied, admiring her poise.

"I am here on Dr. Lifesaver's behalf—he is off today and I am his partner," she said. "How are you feeling today?"

"I'd be better if my infections were under control," I said.

"May I take a look?" she asked.

"Yes," I replied, lifting my gown, exposing my infected incisions.

"Well—I see that you still have oozing," she said. "And I know from your chart that your white blood cell count is still very high."

"I know," I interrupted. "And the wound care specialists still haven't been able to find an antibiotic to fight my infections."

"Are you in a lot of pain?" she asked.

"Yes—especially this pain that seems to be deep down in my pelvic area," I answered, pointing to where the pain was.

"Does this hurt?" she asked, placing pressure on the area.

"Yes!" I cried.

"I can see from your chart, they've been giving you Percocet," she said. "Is that helping with the pain?"

"Yes and no," I answered. "They have me on a four hour Percocet regimen—but I swear by the time the third hour rolls around I am dying."

"Hmmm—let me see what I can do about that," she said. "I am going to note in your chart, if your pain is unbearable, you can have another Percocet when you feel the need. You will still be on your regular four hour regimen—this will just give your nurses a little leeway to stray from protocol."

"Thank you," I said, now perked up.

"Can I get some too?" my husband joked.

"I don't think so," she said, smiling at him.

"You're so funny," I said raising an eyebrow at him.

"Well—if you need anything more today, please feel free to call otherwise you two have a good day," she said, and then exited.

Early that evening, my ex-husband brought my kids back to visit. After an hour of catching up—and them running to and from the cafeteria—it was getting late and time for them to leave. I motioned for my boys to come give me hugs and kisses. My teenager was first, followed by my little guy.

"Hi mommy," he purred as he started to climb into bed with me.

"Hi sweetie," I said.

"Mommy?" he asked.

"Yessss," I replied

"I have a question for you," he said.

"Okay," I said.

"Do yoooou thiiiiiink . . . I could stay and spend the night in the hospital with you?" he asked.

"No honey, you're too young—I'm sure they have rules against that," I answered.

"Come on mommy, please," he cooed.

"Honey—there are too many doctors and nurses attending to mommy," I said. "And then, when they need to check my incisions, you would need to be out of the room and there would be no one to watch you."

"Well—what about my step-dad? He could watch me," he argued stubbornly.

He was always quite the negotiator this one—always thinking. I had to give him credit for trying. His brother, his dad, and my husband were now watching our negotiation session—you never knew what this kid was going to come up with next and it was often entertaining.

"No honey," I said. "Your step-dad has to leave early in the morning to go to work. He needs his sleep and he can't be waking up all night to watch you."

At that moment, I thought this would be a convincing counter-argument.

"But mom—that doesn't make sense," he said.

"What do you mean that doesn't make sense?" I asked, awaiting his next volley.

"It's Saturday and my step-dad doesn't go to work again until Monday," he replied—game over.

I laughed—he was right. I had been in hospitals so long I'd forgotten what day of the week it was.

"You're right," I said, giggling. "I'm sorry. I thought it was a weekday—but the answer is still no."

"But mom," he whined.

"No 'but mom's' about it," I said.

"Okay," he said, sliding off the side of my bed.

"I love you," I said.

"Love you too mommy," he said as they exited my room.

"That kid is quite a character," my husband remarked.

"Yes—he is his mother's son," I said.

My husband winked and blew me a kiss—a gesture we often repeated to one another.

Day 11 - Sunday

It was early Sunday morning and my husband had just left to run some errands. I hadn't even received my breakfast yet and a new nurse, who I will call nurse-Ratched walked into my room. Her facial expressions said it all, "B-I-T-C-H!"

"Hello, I am going to be your nurse for today," she said authoritatively.

Nurse-Angel worked Monday through Friday, so it was par for the course that I would have random nurses on the weekends—but this one I would never forget.

"Hi," I replied.

"Looking through your chart—I see that you had surgery four days ago," she said.

"Yes," I said—no small talk with this woman.

"Well—why haven't you been out of your room walking the halls?" she ranted. "You don't need to be here—you are young—and you should be up and around by now!"

"Excuse me?" I said.

"You heard me," she snapped. "You're not going to get better unless you get out of that bed! This is a cardiac unit for heart patients and the elderly who are very sick!"

"I have no idea what you are talking about," I defended.

"You know exactly what I am talking about!" she snarled.

"Did you bother to read the rest of my chart?" I snapped back. "I've been through three surgeries—my white count is through the roof—and I am in dire straits here!"

"Dire straits?" she snapped right back. "We'll see about that!"

I guess I had gone too far telling her I was in dire straits.

"Huh," she puffed as she marched out of my room.

What just happened? I thought to myself. Where did she come from? Nevertheless, I was happy to see her leave.

Breakfast was served just as my mom arrived—just us two girls again. We talked about what was happening and what I'd been through. I explained to her that no matter what I wanted to play nice—I did not want to be thought of as a problem. Consequently, I was uncomfortable talking about any possible next steps until after I was discharged from the hospital. She agreed and not a moment too soon.

In walked one of Dr. TooCool's colleagues who I will continue to call Dr. Old. Apparently, Dr. Old was the weekend on-call doctor for Dr. TooCool. He seemed much older than Dr. TooCool and acted as if he was Dr. TooCool's superior. He also had a noticeably grumpy edge to him, almost angry.

"Morning," he huffed.

"Good morning," I replied.

"Good morning," my mom said.

"Who's this?" he asked abruptly, looking at me as he pointed his clipboard towards my mother.

"She's my mother," I replied softly, trying to disarm him.

Then he silently sat down on a chair across from us. He flipped through the paperwork on the clipboard he was holding—I assumed it was my chart.

A couple of minutes had gone by and he still hadn't spoken a word—the room was uncomfortably quiet.

Then with his head down—now holding the paperwork in a dropped position between his legs—he began shaking his head "no" over and over again. He was obviously very irritated about something.

Finally he spoke and blurted out loudly, "Pussies!"

I immediately looked over at my mother who was mortified by Dr. Old's outburst—she hated that word. All the same, she saw my pleading eyes and stayed silent along with me. Now, she too, was just sitting there in silence staring at the floor.

Finally, he left without another word.

"Sorry mom," I said.

Shortly afterwards, mom and I finished our visit. She was off to do some shopping for me. Due to my incisions I could not wear anything that might rub against them and I would need some loose fitting outfits before I was discharged from the hospital. In the hospital I was fine having been confined to wearing their standard issued hospital gowns and slip free socks.

"Well—you really are quite a mess," nurse-Ratched huffed, startling me.

"I guess you read my chart," I said.

"Of course I read your chart," she said, again irritated.

"Sorry," I said.

"It's time to clean and redress your wounds," she said. "You can make it to the bathroom and give yourself your own sponge bath, can't you?"

"Yes—and I have been doing that for a couple of days now."

"Good!" she huffed.

I felt like I had been moved to the Prison ward.

"Lift your gown," she ordered, armed with saline and gauze for my wounds.

I complied and neither one of us said another word until she was finished.

"Here's a clean gown," she huffed. "I am sure you can change yourself."

"Yes—thank you," I said.

"I suppose you want your Percocet now too," she asked, handing me a Percocet.

"Yes—thank you," I answered.

Then as she was about to leave, I realized I had to do the unthinkable. I had to stop her and ask for water. I was out and I needed water to take my pill.

"Wait—wait—could I please get some water?" I asked. "I am out and I will need some to take my pill."

"Of course you are out of water," she said. "Anything for attention, I am sure."

"I'm sorry," I said.

"What do you mean, you—are—sorry," she ranted.

Apparently I had hit a nerve again.

"You'll get your water," she said as she walked out the door.

Then amazingly, I heard her yelling at one of the volunteers working at the hospital to "fetch" me some water.

What was wrong with this woman? Had she just stepped out of the Cuckoo's Nest—nurse-Ratched indeed! Just as I was beginning to stress out about how my day was going—my husband walked into my room. I was so happy to see him. Once again at peace, I decided to take a nap and try to sleep through my day—avoiding the wrath of nurse-Ratched.

My middle brother and his significant other were back from their yearlong—out of state—venture and now they were here visiting me. Like everyone else in the family, they were very concerned for my well-being. I tried to reassure them that I was going to be fine. I told them that I still needed one more surgery before I would regain full use of my left leg. They were very supportive and wanted to be present for that surgery. I agreed.

Mom and dad had arrived with my oldest son, followed closely by my two younger sons and their dad. It was like a party, but I was mainly an observer. I was still in a lot of pain and had no energy to participate. But it was nice to see them all and watch them catch up.

Suddenly, my door was slammed shut by someone outside. I guess we were being a little too noisy. So we all agreed to tone it down and were quieter—for a while. Unintentionally, I am sure our noise level slowly crept back up. With so many of us in the room, trying to stay quiet would not be easy. We were always big on family gatherings.

After a couple of hours, all the visiting had exhausted me, so I sent a subtle hint—party over. Again, everyone had left and it was just my husband and I. He was lying on his cot reading his fourth novel while I rested in my bed—mentally working on getting better.

130

Dire Straits

Tonight would be a noisy one. It had always been comforting for me to have the door open. But tonight they had brought in an elderly woman—who didn't want to be there. Apparently, her daughters, due to heart problems had brought her in. I listened as her doctor and what sounded like her daughters were trying to convince her that she needed a pacemaker. But the woman was beside herself, obviously terrified at the thought of undergoing heart surgery.

Her room was directly adjacent to mine. With both doors opened, along with the positioning of our beds, we could barely see into one another's rooms. As I looked over, I noticed that her room was large and was shared by two other patients—apparently other heart patients as well.

Finally, after several hours of her none stop moaning and constant negotiation with her daughters and doctor, I had had enough. I called nurse-Nightwatch—she was back from the weekend—and asked if she would close my door. Peace at last I thought, and without any further interruptions I was able to quickly fall asleep.

Day 12 - Monday

It was Monday morning and this morning would be no different than most. I awoke at about 6:00 a.m. and Dr. X had once again snuck in. Yet this time, instead of being my normal obedient self, I was defiant. Not only was I miserable from the pain I was in—I was irritated by Dr. X's constant uninvited visits.

"Good morning," he said.

"Morning," I replied.

"So has your status changed?" he asked anxiously.

"No—it seems like I am getting worse," I replied. "It's been too long and my infections are continuing to worsen. My white count is still rising and the wound care specialists have not been able to find an antibiotic to fight my infections."

He lowered his head to a downward position, which he maintained and stayed silent.

I was irritated with him. He was the direct cause of everything I was going through. Yet in spite of that, he still had the audacity to continue showing up uninvited—without "hospital privileges"—to pump me for whatever information he could. His actions seemed very self-serving on his part.

"I've even been told that my situation is starting to look grave," I added carefully—I didn't want to expose anyone at Dr. TooCool's hospital; however, I did want to sort of stick it to him at the same time.

He nodded one more time and then turned around and left as he had always done.

That morning, nurse-Angel was back too. And as she had done every morning, she reported to me what my white blood cell count level was—seemingly always on the rise. Except this morning, she would report that my numbers had not changed—this was both good and bad news. The good news was that my white count seemed to have stabilized. But the bad news was that my wounds were still festering with major infections. And on top of that the aching from whatever was causing the deep pain to one side of my pelvis was still severe.

In fact, this pain was unbearable without the Percocet every four hours. It was so bad, it caused me to watch the clock for my next round of Percocet. As soon as four hours had gone by, if no one had come with my Percocet, I would call to have one administered.

Unfortunately, since the weekend had come and gone, Dr. Feelgood's orders were no longer in effect. I was back in the care of Dr. TooCool's orders. As a result, I would not be able to request a Percocet sooner than the four-hour intervals—even if I did feel like I needed it.

As nurse-Angel and I were going through our early morning routine, she pointed out that I still had blood in my urine—in my catheter bag— this too was a real concern. So as she did every morning and late afternoon, she would empty my catheter bag, measure my output, and document the same in my chart. Then a sample of my urine would be sent to the lab for testing. Later, I would research "blood in the urine implications" and have provided my findings herein.[22]

Shortly after breakfast the phone rang. It was my boss this time. This was the first time I had spoken to him since I had left work for my "routine hysterectomy." Up until now my husband had been in touch with him on my behalf.

We caught up, discussing my condition and upcoming surgery. He seemed genuinely concerned so I didn't feel any pressure to get back to work too soon. He updated me on the company and mentioned a few projects he wanted me to work on upon my return.

In the meantime, he understood that after my next surgery, I would require more time off. He had hired a temporary attorney in my absence. Finally, we discussed where my new office would be at the company's new location.

Dad was back and this time he had mom with him—now that she was officially retired. The days were long and very boring, but still my family would stay with me—pretty much around the clock. Likewise, around 6:00 p.m., my husband would return from work and relieve my parents. Tonight he had brought with him our lease renewal contract that I would need to sign as well. Still having no energy, I set down the manila envelope on my bedside table. My parents left and I said goodnight to my husband, who had now settled in and was reading again. Silently I prayed and had a long talk with God—recapping and asking for strength.

Stabilized

All through the night I had kept my door closed. The woman across the hall was still moaning annoyingly. Her daughters were still negotiating with their mother obnoxiously loud. Consequently, with the door closed my room felt more like a coffin, which was why I preferred it open. Nonetheless, with all the commotion outside of my room, it too was causing me to become anxious and filled with anxiety. So I chose the lesser of two evils and asked that my door be closed for the evening.

Day 13 - Tuesday

Something startled me and I was awake. It was Dr. X. He was back again—this guy would not give up.

"Sorry if I woke you," he apologized.

You had to give him credit—he did have an incredible bedside manner.

"It's okay—you just startled me for a minute," I said.

"So how are you doing today?" he asked. "Is there any news on your condition?"

"Actually—yes," I replied. "After you left yesterday morning, I got my white count numbers and my numbers seem to have stabilized at twenty."

"That's good news," he said hopefully.

"Yes," I said. "And I'm supposed to be meeting with Dr. TooCool today to discuss the possibility of scheduling my next surgery."

Then out of the blue, nurse-Nightwatch walked in. Dr. X was clearly startled and he immediately exited—again without saying a word. Odd—he never extends a goodbye—he just disappears as quietly as he comes in.

A man of his word, Dr. TooCool arrived right on schedule.

"Good morning," he said.

"Good morning," I replied with a smile.

"Tell me how you're feeling?" he asked.

"Not much different, but I was informed—yesterday—my white count had stabilized at twenty," I answered.

"This is good news," he said. "Although it is still too high—I'll make you a deal. If you can get your white count, down to ten, I have a surgery opening Thursday morning."

"Great!" I said. I was ecstatic with his news.

"In preparation—I am going to schedule another CT scan for the evening before surgery," he said. "But this time—we will do it with contrast dye."

"Great!" I said, still enthusiastic.

"See you then," he said as he too was smiling as he exited my room.

I was not sure why, but there was no doubt in my mind that I would achieve this milestone. Then, just for a second, I wondered to myself why I had this conviction; moreover, why I had always had this conviction. Then I stopped myself and silently scolded myself for even considering questioning the Holy Spirit that lives inside of me.

Over the next couple of days, I continued my regimen of breathing exercises, pull-ups, healthy eating, and getting out of bed periodically each day. I would do these things, even though I was in constant pain—not sure if the pain had to do with my infected incisions or otherwise. Regardless, I would also spend hours resting and sleeping along with having the periodic upbeat conversation with God—our Lord Jesus Christ.

Later that afternoon, Dr. Lifesaver arrived to check on me. He was aware that I was still experiencing a lot of pain on one side of my pelvis and he was concerned. This was where he had implanted my ureteral stent during my lifesaving surgery. However, due to all my infections the pain could not be pinpointed.

"Good afternoon," he said energetically.

"Good afternoon," I said.

"How are you doing today?" he asked.

"Better—now that I know my white count has stabilized and Dr. TooCool agreed to do my surgery on Thursday if I can get my white count numbers down to ten," I explained.

"That's good news," he said.

"Still—this pain deep down in my pelvis is killing me," I complained.

"Well—it could be caused from the stent if that area too has gotten infected," he said. "But I really don't want to remove the stent yet. It was threaded in your damaged ureter tube which is connected to your bladder in order to keep the tube from collapsing. If we remove the stent and your ureter tube collapses, it will cut off waste flow to and from your bladder."

"I understand," I interrupted.

"Okay," he said. "So I really want to leave the stent in for the full four months before removing it."

"What about the blood still in my urine?" I asked.

"Looking at your chart, there is blood in your urine, but the volume has been improving," he said. "Some blood in the urine is completely normal after the complex surgical procedures you have been through. Your urine output has been extensive—so this too is encouraging news."

"My mom mentioned that you said that I had a lot of scar tissue on my bladder when you made the repairs," I mentioned. "Dr. X said my hysterectomy was to remove my fibroids and a large cyst. Yet afterwards he said I had endometriosis. I'm clueless when it comes to anatomy and confused. What happened to me?"

Dr. Lifesaver explained in great detail about endometriosis and the scar tissue caused as a result—as well as how fibroids and cysts come into play. Later I would research these areas and provide my findings herein.[23/24/25/26]

Following his explanation, he checked my "JP drains" still hanging from my sides. He noted that although there was still some drainage, the amounts were minimal, but he still wanted to leave them in place until just before my discharge. Finally, he examined my incisions and removed the last staple at the "T" where his and Dr. X's surgeries connected.

Later that afternoon, my middle brother and his significant other stopped by to visit; however, only my brother would stay with me. His partner had trouble being in hospitals—the environment freaked him out. So my brother and I caught up. It had taken them seven days to drive cross-country back to his home here with their animals in tow. Movers would follow later in a few weeks with his furniture and cars. He was very happy to be home.

My brother, often the jokester of the family, was able to get me laughing and my mind off of my pain. After a half hour or so, mom and dad were back along with my husband. I guess they had arrived simultaneously walking to my room together. They were happy to see me and my brother chatting away and me in good spirits.

I quickly updated everyone with my news that my white blood cell count had finally stabilized and that Dr. TooCool had been by. I told them he would do my leg surgery Thursday morning if my white count was at ten. Everyone was happy with the news—things were looking up.

A few minutes later, dinner was served and before I knew it, it was gone. I must have been really hungry—I thought to myself. Subsequently, I must have made everyone else hungry too, because now my family was off to the cafeteria for dinner of their own. As they were getting on their way, I asked if they could bring me back some frozen yogurt. Of course they said yes—I was hooked.

Later that evening it would be just my husband and me again. I was in very good spirits and decided that I wanted to spend much of the night sleeping—as I thought this was healing. Nonetheless, just before I was ready to fall asleep, I once again silently prayed to God—this time I had a much longer conversation with Him before falling asleep. My husband of course stayed the night—now reading his fifth novel by David Morrell.

Antibiotic Bliss

That evening I was awakened by nurse-Nightwatch.

"Hey—hey—wake up," she whispered excitedly, smiling from ear to ear.

"What?" I asked softly. "What?"

"They did it—they did it!" she exclaimed.

"What!?!" I asked, joining in her enthusiasm.

"Our wound care lab!" she said. "They found an antibiotic to fight your infections! And I am the one that gets to administer your first dose!"

"Thank you—thank you!" I shrieked. "Thank the guys in the lab for me too please!"

"Thank you God!" I exclaimed as I looked up to the ceiling.

Still smiling, she injected the antibiotic into my central line.

"Honey—honey—wake up!" I said excitedly.

"Huh—huh," he said.

"Wake up!" I continued to shriek. "Great news, they found an antibiotic for my infections!"

"You're kidding me!" he shrieked back, as he too was happy and joining in our excitement. "I can't believe it! I am so relieved."

"Me too—can you please call mom and dad?" I asked. "I know it is late (11:00 p.m.) but I'm sure they're not sleeping very well. But some positive news for a change might help them finally get a good night's rest."

"Sure," he said. "Just give me a second—so I can go pee and find my cell phone to call."

I was a little annoyed that he had to pee first, but I decided not to say anything—patience was not always a virtue of mine.

After he returned from the bathroom, he called my parents and they too were thrilled. And shortly thereafter we all went back to sleep.

Day 14 - Wednesday

I continued my regimen of eating, exercising, and being in good spirits. I was still very weak and fragile, but I already felt like I was getting better. I wasn't sure if it was physiological or something else—or because I had received my first dosage and it was already working. Again, I wouldn't question it. I'd just stay happy.

Before my husband left for work that morning, I asked him to call my oldest son with the good news. Then I quickly called my ex-husband, I wanted him to report the news to my two youngest sons before they left for school. I felt they too needed some encouraging news from their mommy. I figured my parents would take care of spreading the news to the rest of our family and friends.

Nurse-Angel was now on shift and we too shared in my good news. She was further excited to report to me that my white blood cell count was at seventeen—the lowest it had been since arriving at Dr. TooCool's hospital. It seemed the news just kept getting better and better.

Later that morning, I heard a knock at my door. It was nurse-Mother and she too was smiling.

"Hi there," she said, walking into my room.

"Hi," I said, still beaming.

"I heard the good news," she said.

"I know—I am so relieved," I said.

"I was almost ready to ask if we should get you your own mailing address—here at the hospital—since it seemed that you had taken up residence with us," she joked.

"Funny—that's a good one," I said.

"Well—keep up the good work," she said.

"I will, thanks," I said.

Everyone seemed upbeat. It looked like I had beaten the odds—once again—and soon my infections would be under control and I'd eventually be well again.

Then, out of the clear blue, it hit me. I was sitting in bed and suddenly had an urge—for the very first time—I wanted to watch my soap opera. I had not had the energy or focus to even consider watching television until now. This had to be another positive sign.

So I quickly checked the time and realized my show would be on in twenty minutes. I situated myself in bed and pulled the television towards me for the first time—it hung on a long moveable metal arm from the wall—turning to channel five. It was on and I was watching and enjoying it. I didn't feel tired and wasn't having any trouble concentrating. I was thrilled.

Yes, one of my guilty pleasures in life was—and is— the Bold and the Beautiful. I call this my sixteen minutes of indulgence, five days a week. It keeps me in check—at least that's my story and I am sticking to it.

A bit of a workaholic, I often work morning through night not even realizing it until I'd notice it getting dark outside. Many times I had come to realize that I had not even taken time out to eat. Consequently, I'd find myself starving. So I started this ritual—taking time out to watch my guilty pleasure—to keep me in check.

Each weekday at noon I'd turn on the local news while preparing my lunch. Then, at 12:30 p.m., I'd sit down and relax while eating my lunch and watching my show before going back to work. It was a balancing technique I had put in place to ensure that I was taking time out for myself—eating, relaxing, and breaking up the day.

Later, after watching my show, I asked myself, "What else might I do that I hadn't had the energy or desire to do before?" I had packed a stack of fashion books that I was reading, but still hadn't touched them. I looked to my bedside table where they had taken up residence.

I pulled one—The Beautiful Fall: Lagerfeld, Saint Laurent, and Glorious Excess in 1970s Paris—but I wasn't interested. I pulled a second one—The House of Gucci: A Sensational Story of Murder, Madness, Glamour, and Greed—still no interest. So I switched it up, pulling one of my subscription magazines instead that I had brought—Vogue Italia (Italian Vogue), and then Vogue Paris (French Vogue)—yet still no interest.

I looked to the table again and saw a spiral notebook that I had packed. I never left home without a notebook. I used them to record any thoughts or ideas that might pop into my head regarding the launch of our upcoming company. Using this ritual, I rarely missed an opportunity that I may have otherwise missed from not writing down my thoughts as they came to me.

This particular notebook was a girlie-girl notebook—by Monsieur Z. The cover had an animation of a chic woman with long hair, wearing a short yellow dress and white boots. It was appropriately titled, Ultra chic.

I felt different this time—I wanted to open my notebook. So I opened it and began to review my notes inside. I had titled the first page, Fall Collection Ideas, and I reviewed my handwritten list following the title. These were early ideas, the concept phase for our company. But I found I wasn't interested in writing in the notebook.

Then, before putting the notebook down, I contemplated starting a journal—to record my experiences following a botched "routine hysterectomy." Hysterectomy for fibroids and cyst, really was endometriosis or complicated by an extreme case of endometriosis? I figured this was perfect timing as my thoughts were still fresh. But then I quickly decided that this might be a dangerous activity since I was not out of the woods yet. Instead, I closed the notebook and placed it back on the table with my other books.

I was tired again, so I did not fight it. I closed my eyes and took a nap— just as my body was dictating.

After my nap, nurse-Angel checked in and told me that my white blood cell count was now at fifteen—more great news. I was now completely confident that I would be ready for surgery tomorrow morning. My anxiety turned to excitement. Moreover, my husband and parents would finally see an end coming—my nightmare, when death knocked at my door, would soon be over.

So once again I prepared for a CT scan—no food or hydration, not even water until after surgery. That meant no dinner, but I was allowed ice-chips this time—sparingly. After my previous experiences—I got smart too—I was armed with a tube of lip balm for parched lips and upcoming dehydration. I kept this tube in the top pocket of my hospital gown.

Later, the CT lab technicians were back to take me to my scheduled CT scan appointment. This time with contrast dye and another needle jabbed into the back of my hand. Yet I wasn't bothered by the procedure. I knew it was all part of the preparation for tomorrow's surgery—and my eventual discharge.

Bypass Graft Implant

That evening, after another long talk with God—asking for my white blood cell count to be down to ten tomorrow. I slept soundly for the first time. I knew they were still monitoring me—drawing blood and taking my blood pressure every few hours—but I didn't remember a thing. Not sure if it was out of pure exhaustion or if I had finally become immune to all the constant prodding.

This time my husband would not only spend the night with me, he would also stick around the next morning. With surgery scheduled for tomorrow, he had taken the day off so he could be at my side as usual. My parents, oldest son, brother, and his significant other would be present as well before and after my surgery.

Day 15 - Thursday

That morning I woke up to nurse-Angel pre-prepping me for surgery—she was elated.

"Good morning," she said.

"Good morning," I replied.

"Your white blood cell count is at ten!" she reported enthusiastically.

"Great," I said.

"The orderlies are on their way to wheel you to surgery," she continued.

I was happy—but it was a moot point—it had never crossed my mind that my white count wouldn't be at ten this morning. So I was not nearly as excited as nurse-Angel.

Still, this morning was different. Although I was happy to hear that my white count was at ten; for the first time—even before my hysterectomy—a rush of fear overcame me. I couldn't hold back the tears. I was extremely nervous.

The orderlies had arrived and were preparing to wheel me to surgery. Again my catheter bag was thrown in my lap. I was disconnected from the machines with the exception of the IV which would stay connected and follow me to surgery.

As they wheeled my bed through the doors, hallways, and elevators—I was wheeled through a window area. And I thought to myself, "Was this the last time I would ever see outdoors again? Was grandpa there? Was Jesus there?" As I took in the trees and sky, I was truly scared for the very first time and couldn't control my emotions. I was silently praying and outwardly balling.

Finally I arrived in Pre-Op and was greeted by more nurses and staff. They were hooking up my IV with new drugs as I was being shaved (down there) once again. Shortly after my husband and parents were allowed in—one final visit before surgery. While awaiting surgery, my oldest son arrived, but my brother and his significant other still had not. Soon, Dr. TooCool arrived.

"Good morning," he said.

"Good morning," I replied, visibly shaken.

"Your white blood cell count is at ten and we don't anticipate any problems," he said. "Surgery should take one to two hours at most."

He once again followed protocol, showing me the arterial femoro-femoral bypass graft that would be implanted in me. He then removed it from its sterilized container and placed it on the table next to me—a medical cart on rollers. Later, I would research "arterial femoro-femoral bypass grafts" and I've provided my findings herein.[27]

This was the second time I had been through this procedure with Dr. TooCool. I assumed this was protocol and that anytime such a device was to be implanted, the doctor would show the patient the device to confirm it was original and had not been tampered with.

I wondered for a moment, why my husband and parents were so gullible believing Dr. TooCool's story about my previous surgery—it being exploratory and all. Then it dawned on me, they were not in the room when he had gone through this protocol procedure with me before—showing me the vascular graft device in my room.

This would later become a cover up on Dr. TooCool's part. He would either have to absorb the cost of the first bypass graft—which had to be scrapped—or he would have to convince the insurance companies to pay for two. Later, I decided not to pursue my curiosity as to how Dr. TooCool decided to handle his dilemma.

Finally—still upset and scared—it was almost time for me to be wheeled into the Operating Room. My husband and family were escorted out. As I waited alone in Pre-Op; suddenly, I felt a hand gently grab my shoulder from behind. Then I heard the voice of what sounded like a nurse standing behind me: "For this surgery, Dr. TooCool will be assisted," the voice said in a reassuring tone. "Thank you," I acknowledged. Seconds later, the orderlies came into the room and rolled me into the Operating Room—lights out yet again.

At that moment in time and still even today, I am not sure if the touch and words I heard in Pre-Op were actually from a human being or a spiritual being. Either way, the affect of those words gave me an immediate sense of calm and took away all my fears.

Remarkably this surgery was on schedule, lasting less than two hours—the fem-fem bypass was successfully implanted in my groin. As a result, I now had a second vertical incision—three inches long—across from the previous one (four inches long) which they re-opened during this procedure. The graft had been inserted inside my body between these incisions and then connected and sutured to my femoral arteries in each of my legs—re-establishing blood flow to my left leg. Finally, the incisions were sutured closed—no staples this time.

The Beginning of the End

While in Post-Op I was told the surgery was successful. However (always a "however" it seemed), the blood clots had been left in my leg as they were lodged in an unreachable region of my upper leg where they could not be removed. I was reassured that even if one were to dislodge, it would only be able to travel within my limb (leg) and would not be able to travel to my heart or lungs—thus, they were not considered life threatening.

I was so weak and full of pain; I was still trembling after surgery. This fourth surgery felt like it had taken the life out of me. Percocet was no longer going to be able to do the job, the solution: morphine. And now I would have to start all over again, rebuilding strength so I could sit, stand, and walk again.

Out of Post-Op and back in my room, my family quickly joined me. In addition to my husband, parents, and son, my brother and his significant other had also arrived. I was feeling that my brother may have felt slighted since he did not get to see me before going "under the knife" a fourth time. Maybe, I could have asked that they wait for a couple of minutes—but I wanted it over with. Unfortunately, he had arrived seconds after my husband, parents, and son exited Pre-Op and adjourned to the waiting room.

I had no reason to feel guilty and knew my brother would not want me to feel that way either. I was happy the surgery was successful and behind me—I would now have full use of both of my legs. Even though I still had my infections and ultimate recovery to deal with, at least I had peace of mind that I was done with surgery—at least for several years.

A few minutes later, Dr. TooCool arrived and was warmly received by my family and me.

"Well—the operation went flawlessly," he said.

"When will I be able to get out of bed and use my leg again?" I asked, in a rush to move things forward.

"It depends on you," he replied. "With your white blood cell count stabilized and infections under control—as soon as you feel strong enough—you should be able to get out of bed and on your way to a full recovery."

"This is the weakest I've felt since the beginning of this whole ordeal," I said. "And I still have this unbearable pain in my pelvis."

"Well—you have the morphine drip to help you with the pain for now," he said. "But as far as the pain in your pelvis goes, you need to have this conversation with Dr. Lifesaver."

"I am going out of town tonight—so I will not be checking on you tomorrow (Friday) or during the weekend," he said.

"Okay," I said.

"An on-call doctor will be available if you need assistance," he continued.

"Okay," I said.

"In the meantime, I would like you to call my office and schedule a follow-up appointment to see me in two weeks—my office is across the street from the hospital, down the road a bit but not far," he finished, handing his business card to my husband.

"Thank you," I said.

"You're welcome," he said. "I know you've been through a lot."

I was having a hard time with recovery—I was so weak. Just breathing felt like a full time job—even with the oxygen I was being fed through the tubes in my nose, again. It didn't feel like I could breathe naturally anymore. Then anxiety kicked in due to exhaustion. In addition, I found myself extremely irritable—almost to the point of having a full-blown panic attack.

As my anxiety began to consume me—I realized I was having difficulty trying to calm myself down. But I didn't want to tell anyone. Now that I was done with my last surgery I just wanted to get well enough to get out of there and go home.

Then it hit me, I remembered that I was hooked up to a morphine drip. I'd been told that I could have more if I needed it—I needed it! So I called nurse-Angel and asked if I could have another dose. She told me it was okay and I had the controls—so I pressed the button two more times.

Afterwards, I tried to put myself in the calmest state possible. It was working—to a point—but the constant chatter of my family in my room was beginning to annoy me. That was not nice of me, I thought. Still, I needed sleep and solitude. So I told everyone I needed to sleep—but as soon as they left, I felt lonely.

After a nap I felt a little better—at least the anxiety was gone. Yet the one pain deep inside my pelvis was still killing me. Nevertheless, I decided that if I wanted to get out of the hospital morphine was not the answer.

Not to mention, I had no idea what the hype was surrounding morphine. Morphine seemed to just warm the inside of my body and slow things down—especially my heart rate and that concerned me. I never felt high on it. I also knew it was a dangerous drug and I wanted to be done with it.

Now that my surgeries were over, my anxiety had subsided. It was now time for a plan of action. Yes, I always have a plan and if plan A doesn't work, there is always plan B, C, D . . . I am a planner and I love when a plan comes together. I like things in order and I like progress. I have little tolerance for incompetence, so I guess you might call me a type-A personality. And right then, my plan was to get out of Dr. TooCool's hospital before something else happened to me.

It was almost 4:00 p.m. and I knew nurse-Angel would still be on shift, so I rang the call button.

"Hi," I said. "I have decided that I don't want to be on morphine anymore. Instead, I'd like to be put back on Percocet. I'm uncomfortable being on morphine—but I am still experiencing this deep pain in my pelvis and Percocet always seemed to help."

"No problem—your chart still indicates you can have Percocet so I can give you one now and then one every four hours," she said.

"Great—thank you," I said.

"By the way—I won't see you tomorrow," she said. "It's my son's first birthday so I had asked for the day off. But I'll be back on Monday as usual."

"Okay—tell your son happy birthday for me," I said.

"Thanks," she said.

With the help of Percocet, I was able to mask my pain. I didn't want anyone to know how weak I actually was. I wanted one thing and one thing only, to go home. So for now, I would smile superficially and pretend to be well and upbeat in preparation for my discharge.

Today was Thursday and I was not scheduled to be visited by my doctors again until Monday. So my long-term plan was to be out of the hospital before Monday when my doctors would return. My short-term plan, however, was to be out of the hospital and home no later than Saturday.

Time to eat—food had arrived—but I didn't have any desire to eat. But I knew they were recording everything I ate and monitoring my calorie intake. And unless they were happy with my progress, they weren't going to release me.

So—a plan within a plan—I would eat as much as I could to build my strength. Then I would give my dad whatever I couldn't eat, so it would look like I was eating. Dad would oblige and mom would scold dad for eating my food—she didn't know that I was secretly encouraging him to do so. Then, any juices, dry cereals, crackers, and the likes that were leftover, I pulled from the tray and started a bag to hide the food.

Next, I needed to build my strength back. So I attempted to get out of bed before realizing I was much too weak to do so—I nearly fell. Still, no one saw me try so I would just stay in bed and pretend I was just tired.

Okay, now it was time for my breathing apparatus lung exerciser gadget. They recorded how many times a day I did this and how high I could get the lever inside to rise with each breath. So off with the oxygen tubes and I put myself through a couple of reps with the breathing apparatus—now I was light headed.

A little too ambitious I decided—I was exhausted. So again I decided to listen to my body, stop, and relax. My husband had just arrived, and playing tag as he did most nights, my parents now said their goodbyes. Quickly, we caught up with how our days went and then I told him I needed to sleep. He then retreated back to his cot and continued with his reading.

More Anxiety Attacks

The next morning I was assigned to a new nurse who I will call nurse-Yappy—nurse-Angel had taken the day off. And as I would soon find out, I would have my hands full with this one. She was very nice, probably in her early thirties, but she loved to chatter. I mean she never stop talking. There I was trying to keep my anxiety away so I would heal faster—but instead I'd be trapped with nurse-Yappy. I missed nurse-Angel immediately!

Day 16 - Friday

"Good morning," she said.
"Good morning," I replied.

"I am so excited!" she started. "I am going to be your nurse for the next three days. I just got back from maternity leave a couple of months ago and I couldn't wait to get back to work."

"Really," I said trying to sound interested.

"Yes—I just had twins—eight months ago," she said, while draining my catheter bag. "But then I started suffering from post-partum depression on top of my bipolar disorder. Ritalin has saved my life. Now I am back at work and my husband is at home with the twins."

I just smiled. I didn't want to give her any ammunition or reason to keep talking.

"But still I miss my twins," she continued as she wrote her name on the whiteboard. "I am the major 'bread-winner' of our household now so I need to work. My husband got laid off from his job. So I volunteer for three twelve-hour shifts so that I still have four days a week at home with my babies."

"You sound like a very doting mom," I said.

"Actually—after the twins were born—I wasn't that great of a mom," she continued on. I think now she was adding another packet of IV fluids or antibiotics to my IV drip.

Why did I have to speak? I thought to myself.

"I was very depressed and overwhelmed and my doctor's told me I was suffering from post-partum depression," she continued. "This really bothered me and my mom came to stay with us for a few weeks."

Breakfast arrived—thank you, God! She was interrupted for a few seconds.

"I will let you eat your breakfast and then I will be back to clean your incisions and change your bed," she said.

Yikes, I felt my anxiety coming back on. This woman was going to make me crazy—I thought. I knew Ritalin was a prescription drug for

158

hyperactive children, but I had heard that it affected adults differently—like a stimulant. So why would a doctor prescribe such a drug to an adult woman as hyper as this woman?

Here I was still trying to mask my pain, but coupled with nurse-Yappy, it was going to become more and more difficult to do. Nevertheless, I had a plan to execute, so I decided to get out of bed and sit at the desk to eat my breakfast there. I thought this act would look like I was making an effort and show that I was getting my strength back.

BIG MISTAKE! I had just gotten out of bed, dragging my IV rack with me, and flipping my long catheter tube around to get to the desk on the other side of my bed. I had just sat down at the desk, and was ready to pull my breakfast tray over to me, when nurse-Yappy returned.

"What's wrong?" she yelped. "How come you are out of bed? Is something wrong? Can I get you something?"

"No—no—no," I said, while I started to pull my breakfast tray to the desk. "I'm fine."

"Are you sure?" she asked. "Here—let me help you."

"It's okay—I've got it," I said.

"I know but I just want to help," she said, rolling the tray over my catheter tube that was lying on the floor. "Oops—let me fix your bag again."

"Thank you," I said.

"Are you sure you are okay," she asked again.

"Yes—I am fine," I said. "I just wanted to eat my breakfast at the desk instead of in bed."

Now I was feeling pretty proud of myself, thinking I had tricked her into thinking everything was okay—and it worked, she left me alone.

I would be alone this morning until around 11:00 a.m. with nurse-Yappy. My husband was at work and my parents had an appointment. I was miserable and weak. Even though I had been given sponge baths daily, I still felt grubby. My hair hadn't been washed for the last sixteen days. So I was beginning to feel depressed on top of everything else—and it showed. I just finished breakfast and nurse-Yappy was back.

"What's wrong?" she asked.

"My hair is making me nuts—it hasn't been washed in over two weeks," I said.

"Well—we don't have a shower here," she said looking puzzled.

"I was thinking I could sit in front of the sink in the bathroom and wash my hair in there," I continued.

She seemed amused as if no one had ever washed their hair in the bathroom sink at the hospital before. I had my own private bathroom but it was only equipped with a sink and toilet area. Still there was plenty of room to get a chair in front of the sink which could accommodate me. I was still, much too weak, to stand in front of the sink.

"Well—I can bring in some towels, a new gown, and try to find you some shampoo," she said.

"Great—do you think you could find some kind of a cup too so I can pour water over my hair to rinse it?" I asked.

"I'll check around and see what I can find," she replied excitedly.

It seemed like this was a new venture, something that she wanted to be a part of—something different from her day-to-day activities. And together, it felt like we were on a mission.

"Here," she said. "I found some towels—although they are not very big—and I brought you a new gown."

"Thank you," I said.

160

"You just sit there—I am going to move one of these chairs in front of the sink like you suggested," she said.

"Thank you," I said.

"I'll be right back—I am going to see if I can find some shampoo and a pitcher," she continued as she quickly ran out of the room.

While she was out and about, I hobbled to the bathroom, pulling my IV rack along. My catheter bag had a long enough hose to reach the bathroom. However, I quickly found, moving around was not an easy task—especially in my current state of frailness.

Finally sitting down at the sink, I looked in the mirror for the first time in over two weeks. Normally a blonde, my hair now looked dark brown. Weird I thought when I looked in the mirror. I guess after a couple of weeks of not washing my hair, the natural oils had turned it dark.

I had not worn makeup in nearly two weeks either. My complexion looked incredibly smooth and very white, causing my features to look unusually prominent. Maybe it was the lighting I decided. No makeup in my overnight bag, the best I'd be able to do was wash my face with warm water.

"Hi—it's me," she said excitedly. "I've brought a volunteer with me to help."

"Hi—thank you," I replied.

"This is the only thing we could find to use for a pitcher," she explained showing me what looked like a medium size dishpan that you might hand wash dishes in.

"You're not going to be able to do this by yourself," the volunteer chimed in.

So together, the three of us managed to wash my hair—twice—and at the end of the fun we were all soaked. It was a lot of laughs as well—

something I very much needed. My spirits were lifted and I actually had a few minutes where I didn't even notice my pain.

I dried my hair with several more towels as best I could under the circumstances—no blow dryers. I tried to help the girls as much as possible, handing them the wet towels that were surrounding me. They did the rest. I used a large plastic pick that I had brought from home to comb through my hair. Afterwards, I placed my hair back on top of my head and out of the way. My hair was finally clean and I retreated back to bed for a nap—I was exhausted again.

I woke up from a much-needed nap to a pleasant surprise—my parents were back. I told them about my hair washing adventure and they seemed pleased. I also told them I was bored out of my mind and whined about nurse-Yappy. She had been driving me crazy with the exception of the hair washing experience, which I had to admit was very fun.

Throughout the rest of the day, the television was on and my parents were watching cooking channels. I made sure I continued to get in and out of bed, periodically sitting at the desk, so that the nurses knew I was mobile. I also realized that the more I was up and around, the better I felt—it was making me stronger.

Still, I felt my anxiety coming back. Between working to get stronger, hiding my pain, and now nurse-Yappy—I was once again getting anxious. And to make matters worse, the woman across the hall—who didn't want a pacemaker—was moaning again. I felt like I was going to have a full-blown anxiety attack.

I couldn't believe it, that woman was still at it—five days later—still moaning and crying. A doctor and her daughters obviously were still trying to get her to agree to the pacemaker. But she was adamant; she wanted to wait for her own doctor to return from vacation before she would agree to a pacemaker. Yes—I could have shut my door again, but that too would have contributed to my anxiety.

Now one of her daughter's was back in the hall—right next to my room—on her cell phone. She was apparently talking to her sister about their mother and she was obnoxiously loud. She didn't seem to have any respect for any other patients in the ward at the time. And I couldn't figure out why the nurses were allowing her to continue on a cell phone in the hospital—in the Progressive Care ward.

Then—unbelievably—I saw Priest Pester walking into the woman's room. The doctor had left and the daughter was still in the hall next to my room—bothering me—oblivious to what was going on in her mother's room. At first, I thought Priest Pester had gone into her room to try to calm the woman down. But instead—much to my horror—I heard him trying to get a donation from this woman. I couldn't believe what I was hearing—I was appalled by his actions. At this point I had heard enough, I couldn't take it anymore—so I asked my parents to shut my door.

Early that evening, my husband joined us again after he was off work. With everyone together, I told them my plan, to leave the hospital and go home hopefully Saturday. With my infections under control and my being mobile, I figured I could heal just as easily in the comfort of my own home. They were skeptical but would support my wishes.

Loving Friends and Family

Just before retiring for the evening, with my parents gone, I started joking around with my husband. He was on his sixth David Morrell novel now and for some reason I found myself staring at him. He was wearing his reading glasses and he looked just like the Harry Potter character.

"You are so cute—you look just like Harry Potter," I said, giggling.

"What?" he said, now laughing too.

"The way you're sitting there, with your book in hand, and wearing those glasses—you look like Harry Potter," I said.

"Well—if you think I look like Harry Potter—you should take a look at what you look like wearing that scrunchy in your hair," he chuckled. "What would Carrie think?"

He was referring to an episode of "Sex and the City" in which they joked about wearing a scrunchy in public.

"That's mean! I just washed my hair today and that was the only other hair tie I had in my bag," I defended. "I didn't want to put the dirty one back on."

"Sorry sweetie," he chuckled with an evil grin.

"Okay—lights out for you," I said.

"I love you sweetie," he said.

"I love you, too."

Day 17 - Saturday

It was Saturday morning and I had every intention of going home today. So I pushed my call button to call for my nurse—still nurse-Yappy.

"Hi," she said. "What's up?"

"I would like to start the paperwork so I can be discharged today," I said.

"Discharged?" she asked, looking surprised. "There's a lot of paperwork that has to be done before a patient can be discharged—and a doctor would need to sign off on that."

"I understand—but do you think we can start the process for my discharge now?" I asked.

"I don't know," she said. "Let me check with my boss and see what I can do."

Moments later she was back for my daily sponge bath and to clean and redress my wounds. As she worked, she was going on and on about the events of her evening, and how she had to separate her twins into two playpens because one was no longer big enough. But it wasn't a problem, since everyone knew she was having twins, she was gifted double of everything, she continued.

Suddenly, in the middle of our session, in walked one of my dear girlfriends. I was surprised and happy to see her. She immediately realized that I was exposed and offered to wait outside. I quickly said, "No—come in—as long as it's just you and not your husband too." She giggled.

Quickly, the two of us caught up, while nurse-Yappy finished up and tucked me in. My girlfriend was surprised to see the state I was in. Her brother had recently gone through his own ordeal in which after surgery he caught pneumonia and almost died—in a hospital of course.

She told me she had mentioned to him that I was still in the hospital going through my own ordeal, and he was very worried given my length of time in the hospital. He felt—as many others have since expressed—that the longer your time in a hospital is, the worse your odds are for recovery.

"Enough of all that," she said, handing me a gift bag she had been holding dangling from her arm. It was from her and another one of our girlfriend's—a darling two-foot tall black teddy bear. I was very happy to receive such a gift and thanked her.

As she prepared to leave, she apologized for coming against my wishes—my dad told her I did not want any visitors other than family. I assured her not to worry, I was happy to see her and that I considered all my girlfriends family. Shortly afterwards we ended our visit and said goodbye—hugs and kisses.

Just before lunch, I decided that I wanted to read—or at least pretend to read and give the impression I was well enough for discharge. Just in time, nurse-Yappy was back.

166

"Hey there," she said.

"Hi," I said. "I think I feel like reading."

"Really? Great!" she said energetically. "Here—let me help. I'll raise your bed into a sitting position. Then I'll flip this lever so your bed will turn into a chair."

What? I thought. Now she was scaring me and I wondered what the heck I had just gotten myself into.

BANG! BANG!

I heard the bed making loud noises, which didn't sound like normal noises.

"Okay—just one more lever," she said, while she was still working her magic with the bed.

BANG!

"There! See—just like a chair," she said.

"Amazing!" I said—my bed had actually transformed into a chair.

"Thank you."

"You're welcome," she said, obviously quite proud of herself as she left my room.

A couple of minutes later, I found this sitting position very uncomfortable. I yearned for the time when my chair would be transformed back into a bed. But I would fake it for appearances sake.

Around lunchtime, my husband and parents arrived. I told them that I had asked to be discharged today. Based on the looks on their faces, I immediately defended myself. I told them I was bored out of my mind and nurse-Yappy was driving me crazy—I wanted out of there. They reluctantly supported my decision.

At about the same time, nurse-Yappy walked back in. I hoped that she hadn't heard what I had just told my family, "nurse-Yappy was driving me crazy."

"Hi, there!" she said, still full of energy. "I see your family is here too now. Hi everyone!"

"Hi," my husband said.

"Hi," my parents added.

"I wanted to give you an update—we are working on your discharge papers," she said. "But before we can discharge you, we need to arrange with an outside nursing service to come to your home daily to clean and redress your wounds."

"Okay," I said.

"Nurse-Mother has a list of nursing services—she is contacting several now," she said. "They should be faxing us their replies soon."

"What if we don't hear from someone today?" I asked.

"Well that is a possibility," she answered. "And it is the weekend. And I've seen them take days to respond."

I could tell she was about to start babbling again, so I interrupted and asked, "Is there some kind of backup plan we can put in place?"

"Well—if your husband or mother would be willing to clean and redress your wounds—I could teach them how," she said. "But this would only be a backup plan. I'm sure they'll find you someone—they always do . . ."

"Great," I interrupted.

"Honey—you know things like this gross me out—but I will do it if I have to," my husband volunteered.

"That's okay," my mom said. "Of course I can do it until we find a nursing service. It's one of the reasons why I took early retirement, so that I could help with your care until you are better."

"Thank you," I said looking at both of them.

With that settled, we asked the guys—my husband and dad—to leave my room. Nurse-Yappy was about to take my mom and I through the process of cleaning and redressing my wounds—something I had taken for granted until now.

But first, nurse-Yappy needed to morph my bed from a chair back into a bed. With that done, she handed my mom a box of rubber gloves, instructing her to put on a pair. She then walked us through the process, cleaning my wounds with saline and redressing them with gauze and tape. My mom was obviously nervous, afraid she was going to hurt me, and wanted to do it right. But she performed perfectly, despite her jitters.

Just after we finished, nurse-Mother walked in.

"Hi ladies," she said.

"Hi," we replied.

"So—I understand you want to be discharged," she said. "Looking at your chart—I see you've been eating enough. But it's also noted that you haven't been out of your room."

I was looking at her with a confused expression on my face.

"We will not be able to discharge you until we know you are able to walk our halls alone without assistance," she said. "So you won't be going home today."

I was frustrated with her news and lied, "Had I known that I was supposed to be walking the halls I would have been doing so." I could barely walk around my bed without feeling like I was going to collapse.

"I know you are frustrated—but those are our rules," she said.

"I understand—I will begin walking the halls immediately now that I know it's expected of me," I said.

Now what did I get myself into? I thought. But I knew I had to do it. So I smiled, masking my pain, and asked my husband to escort me. Like we were on a date, but not really—he is a big guy so I wanted him next to me in case I fell.

Together we walked outside of my room for the first time. I walked about ten feet and could now see the entire room the moaning woman was in. She was in there with three other patients, not two as I had previously thought. It was a much larger room than the room I was in. And I wondered how her roommates could stand the constant drama—between her, her daughters, her doctor's stand-in, and Priest Pester.

Nurse-Yappy saw me in the hall and noticed the curiosity on my face as I looked into that room. But she assumed—inaccurately—that my curiosity was for other reasons.

"Those are heart transplant and pacemaker patients," she whispered loudly.

"Oh," I said nodding.

Suddenly, I felt like I was beginning to shake and feared collapsing—but I couldn't I thought. I had to do it. So I decided to use the woman's room as a distraction. I told nurse-Yappy it was late and that I would rather walk the halls in the morning—tomorrow. She bought it and somehow I made it back to my bed. I was exhausted.

My parents left for the evening. Now it was just hubby and I again. I whined to my husband about my pending discharge and not being able to go home yet. I didn't mention to him how weak I really was. He hadn't noticed that I could barely walk the halls—I had him fooled too. So I decided to take a few liberties and I begged him to go out to the nurses' station and ask for a status on my pending discharge. I figured the more I pressed, the sooner they would discharge me. He had no problem accommodating me.

Upon his return, he gave me good news! Apparently, the on-call doctor had signed off on my discharge. I was ecstatic and beside myself—I was going home tomorrow! I couldn't wait, so I decided to hurry up and go to sleep so tomorrow—Sunday—would come sooner.

Discharge

That evening, I lied in bed and did a lot of soul searching. I knew that even if I could pull off my discharge tomorrow, I still had a long way to go with respect to recovery. I still had two more open wound infections, a burning pain deep inside my pelvis, and I was trying to gather the strength to walk more than a few feet without feeling like I was going to collapse. Still I wanted to be discharged before my regular doctors were back on shift Monday.

So before closing my eyes to sleep, I had another heart to heart with God. I asked for strength. I told Him I knew that sleep was healing so I was about to do that. I thanked Him that I was alive and assured Him that I knew it was because He still had things for me to do.

Day 18 - Sunday

Sunday morning, I woke up feeling the most rested I had felt since my last surgery. I felt stronger today—so I thought. So I climbed out of bed and walked to the chair next to the desk. Then I sat down and waited for my breakfast, which had become routine for me now.

As I sat there, I realized I was still very weak—even the most miniscule task took great effort. My body still didn't want to sit, let alone walk. But I had to fake it. I had to do what was expected of me. And so, I sat.

Hubby was awake! Hurray a distraction! Happiness turned to temporary disappointment, when he quickly left to take care of business as had become routine for him. Breakfast was served and I began to eat. My husband was back, now joined by my dad. Apparently they had run into each other in the hall and decided to make a detour to the cafeteria themselves—they too were armed with breakfast.

After breakfast, I retreated to bed—for just a half hour or so I told myself. And then nurse-Yappy walked in.

"Hi—let me take that for you," she said, removing my breakfast tray and placing it on a cart outside my room.

"Thank you," I said.

"Well—we received two faxes from two nursing services that can come to your house once a day to tend to your wounds," she gasped. "The only problem is—both agencies only have their answering services available on the weekends, so they won't be able to confirm until Monday."

"That's okay," I said.

My mother walked in armed with shopping bags from Nordstrom. I smiled at her.

"But just in case," nurse-Yappy continued—not even acknowledging the presence of my mother. "I am going to send you home with bags of supplies in case your mom needs to clean and redress your wounds before the nursing service gets back to you."

"Thank you," I said.

"You're welcome," she said with a bounce in her step as she left my room.

Mom and I then gathered around all the Nordstrom bags. She had purchased two nightgowns, a lightweight summer robe, and a black baby doll dress made out of jersey. Everything could comfortably drape over my incisions without pressing against them. I especially loved the little black dress, so my mom mentioned that they had another in brown—she would go back and buy that one too.

Thirty minutes had gone by—so true to my plan, I forced myself out of bed again. I told everyone I was ready to walk the halls; however, this time I would first change into my new night gown and robe, and put on a clean pair of hospital issued slip free socks.

Once again, I asked my husband to escort me—in case I fell. I wasn't taking any chances. He had always been my knight in shining armor and I always felt safe next to him. So with my husband on one side and my IV rack and catheter bag on the other, off we headed.

"Wait—wait—wait," nurse-Yappy yelled.

"What?" I asked.

"Before you start walking the halls, let me remove your catheter for you," she said. "The doctors will be in to disconnect everything else later—but I can disconnect your catheter now."

"Okay," I interrupted. "Just tell me what you want me to do."

"Go ahead and lie back down on your bed," she said.

174

So I lied back down and took a deep breath just as she instructed—while she removed the catheter tube—and it was done. Awesome! I thought. My plan was working and the wheels were in motion—soon I would be discharged.

As I began to walk the halls, I decided to head in a different direction—away from the moaning woman—with my husband and IV in tow. This was the second hardest thing I had, had to do. (The first, when I got out of bed the first time at Dr. X's hospital.)

Now, I was trembling and I was cold so I stayed close to the walls.

I purposely walked past the nurses' station—trying to look strong and put on a good show. Shortly after, I was shaking horribly and having a hard time controlling myself—I thought I was going to fall.

My husband had taken notice this time and asked if he could help. I told him, "No." Then I lied again, "I'm just cold."

He bought it, so I told him I was bored and together we turned around and headed back to my room. I did it! Then, I retreated back into my bed—I was worn out.

It was 11:00 a.m. and I was scheduled to be discharged at 12:00 noon. Dr. Feelgood had just walked into my room. She was the on-call weekend doctor again.

"Good morning," she said.

"Good morning," I said, noticing that my husband had perked up at the sight of her.

"So—I hear you are leaving us today," she said.

"Yes," I said with a big smile.

"Since you are lying down, I am going to go ahead and remove your JP drains," she said.

"Thank you," I said.

Moments later the gross drainage bags were gone and replaced by more gauze and tape—I was starting to feel human again. Next she disconnected my IV and all the connections to my central line.

"Now it's time to remove your central line," she informed.

This was something I was very nervous about. The central line looked like a one-inch square plastic piece with three holes at the top for injections—it was firmly implanted in my upper chest. I feared it was going to hurt when it was removed so I was not looking forward to this part.

"I need you to hold still," she said, while she clipped the sutures on each corner of the central line that were holding it in place. "Now take a deep breath."

As soon as I had taken a deep breath, she quickly pulled it out, pressing gauze over the holes to stop the bleeding. She then taped the gauze down. I was amazed—it didn't hurt, although it felt a little uncomfortable but it didn't hurt.

"All done," she said.

"Thanks," I said. "That didn't hurt at all."

"You're welcome," she said with a smile.

"Honey look—no more hook ups. You're free," my mom said cheerfully.

"Here is a prescription for Percocet—she will need it when she gets home," Dr. Feelgood said, handing my husband the script. "There is a pharmacy down the hall—you can have it filled there before she is discharged."

"Thanks," my husband said.

Then I noticed an odd smirk on his face as he headed out the door.

"Well—that's all," she said. "Take care of yourself. You will be well again soon."

"Thank you," I said as she walked out the door.

Moments later my husband returned with my prescription for Percocet. I asked him what the smirk was about. He told me he had read the script and couldn't believe it—it was for one hundred pills, enough for both of us he joked. Now I was smirking too, Percocet had been like a lifesaver to me. Often it had been the only thing that would take the edge off the pain I was constantly in.

Finally, it was time to pack, clean up, and say goodbye. My husband and mom gathered my personal belongings—and the food I had stashed in a bag. They also gathered the several bags of supplies nurse-Yappy had packed for me. It took several trips back and forth to their cars. Nurse-Yappy was back to help out, as she happily continued chattering.

"What about the hospital socks?" I asked.

"Oh—you get to keep those," she answered.

"Great!" I said, handing my mother the extra pair to put in the bag she was packing.

"Just a minute," nurse-Yappy said. "I'll be right back."

"Okay," I said, curious as to what she was up to now.

"Here!" she cheered, handing me Wilson (the round yellow smiley faced pillow). It had been signed by several of the nurses from the cardiac unit.

"Thank you," I said appreciatively. I hadn't even missed Wilson—but he was back now and I was happy to see him.

Finally it was noon, and right on schedule a volunteer had arrived with a wheelchair to escort me out of the hospital. My husband was asked to bring our car around and was directed where to pick me up. I kissed my parents and thanked them. My trip home would be just my husband and I—as I had requested. My parents were exhausted too and I'm sure they also needed a break.

Then, as the volunteer pushed me through the hospital halls and corridors towards the exit, I noticed it was a very long route. People were staring at me but I didn't care. I was happy to see plain clothed strangers for the first time in nearly three weeks. Still, for most of the ride, I kept my head down as I was still very weak and exhausted—I needed a quiet mind.

When we arrived at our car, the volunteer and my husband helped me into the car. I held Wilson firmly in front of my abdomen as my husband buckled me in. It was a bright sunny day and I wished I had my sunglasses.

Home Sweet Home

On the way home, I tried to stare out the windows and take in the scenery, but my mind began to play tricks on me again. I was so weak I couldn't concentrate. It was as if my eyes didn't want me to be looking at anything moving—so I closed them for the rest of the journey home. Every turn of the car took my breath away. I was still in so much pain—I wondered, was I premature in my discharge?

Finally we arrived, parking in our gated parking garage. My husband helped me out of our car with Wilson in tow. A few feet away, he helped me to the elevator and up we went—four flights. After the elevator doors opened, I still needed to walk another thirty yards or so to our front door. I made it! I was back in my home—my sanctuary.

Then, after entering our apartment, I felt like I was going to die all over again. I started crying. I was in so much pain. I was so weak and I didn't know what to do. I frantically called my mom. She told me, her and dad would be right over.

I asked my husband for another Percocet—I was now taking two at a time. I couldn't bear the pain and I didn't have the security of being in the hospital if anything went wrong. So I made a call to the nurses' station at the hospital. Frustrated, the only advice I received was that I could re-admit myself—something I was not willing to do.

I slowly made it to our bedroom, holding onto walls and furniture as I made my way to bed. I was balling and lied down to wait for the Percocet to kick in and take away some of my pain. Then as soon as I lied down the doorbell rang—my parents had arrived. Mom came into my bedroom and asked what she could do. I told her I didn't know and that I was going to try to take a nap.

Well that didn't work, ten minutes later and I was still awake—not able to sleep because of the pain I was in. I managed to stand up again and asked my husband for Dr. Lifesaver's phone number. I remembered that Dr. TooCool had told me the pain deep in my pelvis was probably due to the stent Dr. Lifesaver had put in during surgery.

So I called Dr. Lifesaver's office to explain the pain I was in. His answering service answered and said they would page him. Several minutes later, he called and agreed to see me the next morning—Monday morning. Having an appointment scheduled seemed to help me psychologically—knowing something would be done about my pain.

I knew my parents were exhausted and there was really nothing they could do, so I sent them home. I assured them that between my husband and I, we could clean and redress my wounds. It was only around 2:00 p.m. that afternoon and I would not have to clean or change my wounds until around 5:00 p.m.

We lived in a gated community in a beautiful apartment complex, surrounded by lushly landscaped gardens and warm adobe architectures. No stairs inside, we had two bedrooms, two bathrooms, a laundry room, kitchen, living room, and dining room. Our balcony overlooked the grounds and its large pool and Jacuzzi.

While in the hospital, our lease had come up for renewal. Although my husband had signed and renewed it, the manila envelope with blank signature pages for my signature were still waiting for me on the dining room table. And now Percocet had kicked in a bit so I managed to make it to the dining room table and signed the paperwork for my husband to return to the leasing office.

Our apartment was exactly how I left it—a mess. This too made me feel ill. My normal routine was to have an immaculate house at all times. But in the weeks leading up to my surgery, I had deteriorated so badly, I had no energy to do housework. I was barely making it back and forth to work. Consequently, the house remained unpicked up and a mess.

My husband, a lifetime bachelor until marrying me three years earlier, had no idea on how to clean—let alone do laundry. As a bachelor, when he needed his apartment cleaned, he would hire a maid service. When his laundry needed washing, he would take it to the dry cleaners nearby that offered "wash and fold" services. He was spoiled, but he worked hard and was paying for these services so I didn't see anything wrong with his lifestyle.

I gave him a break though. After all, he had just spent nearly every night with me in the hospital. While still managing to go to work and take care of any other chores that could not wait for my return—renewing our lease. So I could not possibly have expected him to find the time to clean house. He had his priorities right—taking care of me at the hospital.

Not to mention that it was my lifestyle that required an immaculate house, not his. I had hired housekeepers in the past and usually found them good in the beginning. But often, once they got comfortable I was less than satisfied. Not only would their work become unacceptable over time, but also some would bring others with them to assist—or worse just to hang out. Thus, since it was primarily just my husband and I—I opted to handle my own household affairs.

It was around 5:00 p.m. and time for me to work with my husband to clean and redress my wounds. I washed my hands and removed my bandages while standing in front of our mirrored closet doors. Then I lied down on our bed with my wounds fully exposed so they could be cleaned. My husband washed his hands before putting on a pair of sterilized gloves. He pulled out the saline solution, the gauze, and now he was looking for the tape. Suddenly we realized—there was no tape to redress my wounds—it must still be in a bag in my parents' car.

I quickly called my mom and told her our dilemma. She placed me on hold while she checked her car. Sure enough, she still had another bag in her car with the tape and more supplies. She felt terrible and said she would be right over. I felt bad that she—once again—would have to make yet another trip to our apartment. But we had no choice as we didn't want to take any chances.

Mom arrived and diligently tended to my wounds—saved by the mother-in-law, my husband was relieved. He never really wanted to do it anyway, but he would have if I needed him to. I thanked my mom and she once again headed downstairs where dad was waiting in their car to take her home.

Finally, my husband and I were lying in our own bed, in our apartment, alone for the first time since our nightmare began. I would spend the next couple of hours moaning and silently crying while tears of pain rolled down my face. I was still in so much pain and I was scared not knowing what was causing it. Not sure if it was out of pure exhaustion or an answer to my prayers, but I was able to fall asleep and sleep through the night.

The Culprit

It was Monday morning and my parents had offered to take me to my appointment with Dr. Lifesaver so that my husband could go to work. My appointment was at 10:30 a.m. and my parents promptly arrived at 9:30 a.m. Still feeling too weak to get dressed I would go to this appointment in a nightgown and robe. Dad drove and I asked to sit in the backseat—movement still seemed to bother my eyes and general well-being. So I sat in the backseat with my head down in silence.

Apparently, Dr. Lifesaver had two offices, and today's appointment would be at his office adjacent to Dr. X's hospital. Upon arrival, dad helped me out of the car. The sun was extremely bright and again I wished I had brought my sunglasses. As I slowly walked into Dr. Lifesaver's office, I waited in the reception area. It was a very elegant and contemporary office setting; the waiting room was a long corridor with chairs lined up on one side and artwork encased in glass on the other side. My mom went ahead to the reception area and told the receptionist that I had arrived for my appointment.

A few minutes later, a nurse greeted us and asked that we follow her. She took us to a small conference room filled with bookcases and anatomy related gadgets. Question and answer pamphlets were also on the table. In the center of the conference room table was a model of the female anatomy and surrounding organs for demonstration purposes. Unlike a regular conference room, this one was built with a four-foot internal wall that led into the exam room on the other side—again feeling very contemporary.

My dad and I studied the various gadgets while waiting for Dr. Lifesaver. My dad tried to keep the conversation light and added a few antics of his own to lighten the mood. I was sure he felt uncomfortable too, but he was happy to be there with me. My mom brought a book and had just started reading when Dr. Lifesaver came in and greeted us.

After a general discussion, Dr. Lifesaver led me behind the four-foot wall into the exam room. My parents stayed in the conference room area where they could hear but not see my exam with Dr. Lifesaver. This was great—I thought—as I would not have to update them later.

Upon examining me, Dr. Lifesaver still thought my pain was just a side effect of healing and wanted to keep the stent in place. I reluctantly agreed and he gave me a prescription for yet another antibiotic. I mentioned that at times, I needed to take two Percocet's and feared running out with all the pain I was experiencing. So he wrote me another prescription.

By now it was nearly noon and I was starving; so I asked my parents if we could stop at a fast food drive through. I knew there was no food at home and they happily agreed. During the ride, I called my husband and updated him on my doctor's visit. I also asked him, if he could stop by Dr. TooCool's hospital and pick up the prescriptions Dr. Lifesaver had just phoned in.

After finishing my cheese burger and a small diet coke, we arrived home. My parents followed me to the elevator and back to my apartment. My mom tucked me in—this time on my couch—in a position where I could keep my leg up which seemed to help with my pain. She then decided she would go back to Nordstrom, to purchase the brown baby doll dress since I had liked the black one so much. After she left, I handed my dad the remote and together we watched "Cesar Millan's Dog Whisperer" followed by court reality shows.

Mom returned around 4:00 p.m. with dress in hand and I thanked her. My parents stayed another hour so she could clean and redress my wounds at 5:00 p.m. again. We still had not heard from any of the nursing services that the hospital had supposedly arranged. Meanwhile, my mom cleaned our kitchen and picked up the clothes scattered around our bedroom floor.

Shortly after my mom had finished cleaning and redressing my wounds, my husband arrived, relieving my parents for the day. Once my parents were gone, my husband and I caught up. He was happy that I was bold enough to ask for another script of Percocet. He knew I didn't like taking pills and more than likely there would be many left over after my infections were healed. He liked having them on hand after a night out drinking—the ultimate hangover cure he joked.

Three days had gone by and I was sure the antibiotics should have kicked in by now—but my pain was not getting any better. Again, I called Dr. Lifesaver's office, but was told he was busy and would call me back. I retreated to the living room with my dad—mornings were his shift while my husband was at work. My mom would relieve dad in the afternoons as no one was comfortable leaving me alone. And I appreciated having someone there.

Several hours later, at around 4:30 p.m., Dr. Lifesaver returned my call. Once again I explained that my pain was not getting any better. In fact, it was actually getting worse. He agreed to see me again the next morning and scheduled a 9:00 a.m. appointment. I thanked him and was again relieved.

The next morning, my husband took the day off to escort me this time to my 9:00 a.m. appointment. This time it would be at Dr. Lifesaver's second office location—closer to our apartment. Still not able to wear underwear, I dressed in the black baby doll dress. Once I was dressed, my husband slowly escorted me to our car. And again, I would have Wilson with me to guard against the pressure of the seat belt.

When we arrived, we took the elevator to the second floor where his office was located. As my husband opened the door, I noticed that the waiting area was not very big, much different from his other office. As we walked to the receptionist, I told her we were there for my 9:00 a.m. appointment. She was expecting me and asked us to have a seat.

While waiting in the waiting room I observed that although the room was small it did have all the customary bells and whistles: chairs, books, and a couple of kids play areas. It was warm and calming—you could also tell that many of his patients were probably children based on all the color crayon drawings taped to the walls.

Next a nurse greeted us. She asked us to follow her to a conference room where Dr. Lifesaver would meet with us before my exam. During this meeting, Dr. Lifesaver still wasn't convinced that my pain was being caused by the stent; he still thought it was all part of the recovery process. So he decided to place me on a stronger antibiotic and handed me another prescription. I was frustrated—but what did I know, I wasn't a doctor.

On our way home, we went through a drive through pharmacy to fill my prescription. With new antibiotics in hand, my husband, Wilson, and I arrived home once again. Diligently I read the prescription label and immediately took my first dose. I was to take one tablet twice a day for fourteen days. Moreover, because it was a stronger antibiotic, I would be cautious and allow myself only one Percocet every four hours instead of the two I had been taking.

Four more days had passed and the stronger antibiotics were not helping. I again called Dr. Lifesaver's office. I insisted that the antibiotics were not working and I wanted another appointment. Again, I was told that Dr. Lifesaver was busy and he would have to call me back. Finally at 4:30 p.m.—same time I thought—the phone rang. It was Dr. Lifesaver and he agreed to see me again the next day, late morning.

The next morning, I still was not able to take a shower, only sponge baths but I needed my hair washed. So I mustered as much strength as I could and washed my hair in the kitchen sink—the bathroom sink was much too low in my current state. Then after blow drying my hair, and putting makeup on for the first time since my ordeal, I got dressed—again, in my baby doll dress. This would be the first time Dr.

Lifesaver would see me with my hair down and makeup on—I somehow felt a little better.

My husband again drove me to my appointment with Dr. Lifesaver. This time, instead of the conference room, I was led directly to an exam room accompanied by my husband. Oddly, it seemed his nurse wasn't prepared for what he intended to do during my appointment.

"Hi, there," he said. "So—are you ready to have your stent removed?"

"Yes," I said excitedly—this was news to me as well.

"Please set-up for a ureteral stent removal," he ordered, looking at his nurse who seemed dumbfounded.

"O—Okay," his nursed replied.

"That's what we're here for—right?" he asked warmly.

"Yep," I said with a smile.

"Do you want to watch?" he asked.

"Absolutely not," I said. "But my husband can if he wants."

"Yeah—I want to watch!" my husband answered.

That surprised me. He was normally so squeamish when it came to matters of the anatomy.

"So—how long will the procedure take?" I asked.

"About three minutes," Dr. Lifesaver answered.

A few minutes later, the nurse was back.

"First—I'm going to numb the area," Dr. Lifesaver said.

"Okay—but I hate these things," I said.

"Take a deep breath," Dr. Lifesaver instructed.

And as soon as I took a deep breath he pulled something out of me. It was very uncomfortable—even with the area numbed—but it lasted only a couple of seconds and didn't really hurt.

"Cool!" my husband said. "That looks like a long wire."

189

"Quick—quick—hand me a urine sample cup," Dr. Lifesaver shouted to his nurse. He found the culprit!

"Am I okay?" I asked.

"Yes—but from the color of the urine that leaked from you, it does look like you have an infection," he said. "We will take the sample to the lab and have the results by the end of the day. I will call in a prescription thereafter and your husband can pick it up for you."

Later I would research the "risks associated with stenting" and provide my findings herein.[28]

"Thank you," I said.

"You're welcome," Dr. Lifesaver said.

"Thank you doctor," my husband added shaking Dr. Lifesaver's hand.

After the procedure, I had only experienced mild burning when peeing thereafter. The stent apparently had a small thread attached to it that Dr. Lifesaver used to pull it out. But I was still experiencing the same pain deep inside my pelvis even with the stent removed—more infection.

Later that afternoon, Dr. Lifesaver called me at home and prescribe yet another antibiotic to fight the infection. At least the problem had been pinpointed—so I thought.

After another three days had passed, I continued to be in severe pain. So, once again, I called Dr. Lifesaver's office and I was again told that he would have to call me back—this time he would call me back around noon. He told me that he wanted to refer me to a specialist—a urologist who I will call Dr. Z. I agreed and made an appointment with Dr. Z for the next day.

Again, my husband drove me to the appointment. Dr. Z's office was also close to Dr. X's hospital. Upon arrival, my husband and I sat in a large waiting area. Dr. Z's office was a lot bigger and it was obvious that there were several doctors working within Dr. Z's office. Strange, I thought as most of the patients in the waiting room were men. Later, I learned that men with prostate issues were referred to urologists.

After an initial exam with Dr. Z, he too needed a urine sample and would also send me out for blood work. The next day, I received my results back from Dr. Z. He had come to the same conclusion as Dr. Lifesaver and prescribed more antibiotics.

Finally, a couple of days later—and a lot of prayers with God—my infection began to subside. Not sure if Dr. Z was the one who ultimately found the right antibiotic that would fight my infection to the end, or if Dr. Lifesaver was on the right track all along, or if God had something to do with it. I still had a couple of days worth of antibiotics to take that Dr. Lifesaver had prescribed prior to my appointment with Dr. Z. Had I waited and not made the call until they were gone, would I've needed to see Dr. Z? Anyway, I was grateful that Dr. Lifesaver had taken the added precaution and sent me to a specialist for a second opinion—seeing me through recovery from the infection.

Follow Up

Now that the infection and constant follow-up with Dr. Lifesaver was behind me, I could now concentrate on other things. So I scheduled follow-up visits with Drs. X and TooCool as each had requested. I felt even with the follow-up visits, my ultimate recovery would take years. I also knew that I would never be fully whole again and would have to monitor my bypass graft frequently.

First, I followed up with Dr. TooCool's office. This being the first time I'd see his office. It would also be the first time he had seen me in street clothes, makeup on, and hair down. Like Dr. Z, he too had several doctors working in his practice—at his office across the street from his hospital.

Strange, Dr. TooCool's bedside manner was very different from what I remembered. He seemed uncharacteristically cold and distant, unlike the warm energetic doctor I had known. He seemed annoyed and didn't have much of anything to say to me. He told me that I really didn't need to see a vascular surgeon more than once a year—unless I began to experience problems with my leg.

Needless to say, I got the hint and would not return to Dr. TooCool's office ever again. I was fortunate; although I had been using my PPO insurance through my employer, I had an alternative. I also had my husband's HMO insurance ever since we were married—but I had yet to use the plan. I was under the misconception that a PPO was better than an HMO. Today, I don't think there really is a difference, i.e., at the end of the day, it's all about the doctor—regardless of the type of insurance plan.

Lastly, I scheduled a follow-up with Dr. X. Surprisingly, when Dr. X saw me; he treated our visit like a normal follow-up. There was no recap, no questions or answers presented from either of us. I knew I should have asked all the questions I'd had on my mind—but I could not find the words. Instead, it was just a cordial visit.

He told me that now that I had had a hysterectomy, I could go five years before needing another vaginal examine—unless I felt an infection coming on. He then prescribed Premarin, an estrogen hormone replacement therapy (HRT) pill that he wanted me to take daily, and an ointment of the same for me to use nightly.

According to Dr. X, I'd need the ointment due to my drop in estrogen, which would cause thinning of my vaginal walls creating less lubrication. Finally he finished, handing me a prescription for each and then proceeded to load me up with samples of the same. Again we were cordial and said our goodbyes.

I learned that I had endometriosis all along—not the fibroids and cyst that had been diagnosed—that caused me to need a hysterectomy. I wasn't having a problem with fibroids and a cyst; I was having a problem from my long bout of undiagnosed endometriosis.[29/30/31/32]

Then when Dr. Lifesaver took over Dr. X's surgery, making a ten-inch vertical incision from my horizontal hysterectomy incision—opening me up wider—he found that endometriosis had moved outside of my reproductive organs area and had eaten away a portion of my bladder. Clearly my bladder is not part of my reproductive organs.

So did the botched hysterectomy save my life? If there is no cure for endometriosis, do I still have it? Even if endometriosis is not cancerous, clearly when it moves on to other organs outside the female reproductive organs, organ failure can cause death—albeit endometriosis only an indirect cause of death.

First Year

30

My first year was by far the toughest. Initially, I had to rehabilitate myself to regain my strength so I could resume my lifestyle—unbeknownst to me, it would be a modified lifestyle. Until this first year, I had always taken for granted the simple things in life—walking, breathing, and so forth. I had always been healthy and never really thought about my health. Throughout this first year I would have to face many challenges head on.

After returning home from the hospital I could barely move. In the beginning, I tried keeping my leg elevated as it seemed to feel better that way. My parents loaned me one of their reclining chairs so that I would not have to sit sideways on the couch. Yet after a few days, I felt like the chair was more of a hindrance—cluttering our apartment—

than helping my leg. Clutter and my house not being in order started to pull me into a depression, so I wanted the chair out. My oldest son was kind enough to move the chair to my house and then back to my parents' house.

Shortly thereafter, my aunt (my mom's sister), and uncle with my grandmother (my mom's mother) traveled cross-country in their recreational vehicle to visit. My uncle's mother lived in the area and she was in grave health herself. So while making their rounds, visiting family, I received a surprise visit from them. I hold this visit dear to my heart as this was the last time I would see my grandmother alive—she was ninety-one.

Lying around the apartment, not doing anything—other than catching up on TiVo (our DVR), watching court television shows with dad in the mornings, and chic flicks with mom in the afternoons. It was all taking a toll on me. I knew I had to do something. So the next morning, I talked my dad into walking with me downstairs to a nearby deli for lunch. This was the first time I'd ventured out of our apartment on foot. I needed some normalcy back into my life and that meant being mobile.

Slowly, I made it to the deli—about one-hundred yards from our apartment. Even though I was trembling and thought my legs were going to give out beneath me, I eventually made it. We ordered a couple of sandwiches and decided to eat outside in the fresh summer air. Funny, even eating a simple sandwich was difficult and I could only finish half.

As my dad and I sat outside eating lunch, my mom walked up. She didn't see us upstairs, but she saw dad's car in the parking lot so she knew we couldn't be far—she was not alarmed. Instead she decided to explore my normal stomping grounds and found us. I asked her to join us and gave her the other half of my sandwich.

Lunch was over and that was dad's cue to leave—he was off his watch and it was mom's turn to take over. So, we said our goodbyes to dad. But I wasn't ready to go home, I wanted to savor the moment and do more. I thought about what the wise nurse at Dr. X's hospital had told me the first time I got out of bed—if I returned to bed immediately after taking care of business I would not want to get out of bed again. And so, I wanted to take her advice again. So I told mom I didn't want to go back just yet.

As we left the deli and started walking down the shopping strip, my mother decided she wanted to go into Borders. I told her that I would wait outside and so I sat down on the built-in ceramic bench across from Borders' entrance. While I sat, I decided to call my husband and surprise him with my whereabouts. He answered and was delighted to hear my news. A few moments later, mom returned; and so, I said my goodbyes to my husband.

As mom and I continued up the strip, the gift shop caught my eye. There were several jewelry racks on display. One of which was an accessorized woman in a leopard bikini and lace stockings—she was the stand—but instead of a head, she had a jewelry rack. The two accompanying pieces were shaped like shoes—one large and one small to hold rings. I couldn't resist and told my mom that I was going to buy myself a coming home present. So I did. After buying my present, I was exhausted so we slowly headed back to the apartment.

Finally—something normal—I was walking again. That afternoon I talked to my mom and told her I didn't need round the clock assistance anymore. It had been nine days since my discharge and it lifted my spirits when I realized I wanted to be on my own again—no more caregivers. I enjoyed my solitude and was not use to having people constantly around me—one more step towards normalcy. With that said, mom was happy to be on her way as she enjoyed her own time as well.

Over the next few days, I continued to push myself until I was once again cleaning house and doing laundry—I call this nesting. However, what would normally have taken me a single day, would now take several days. Nevertheless, in just a few days, my house was once again immaculate and this too put a smile on my face; getting things back to normal was what I needed.

After my follow-up with Dr. X, I'd filled my prescription—thirty pills of Premarin (estrogen HRT)—to cover my first month. But after a couple of weeks, I noticed that the pills were upsetting my stomach, which prompted me to research Premarin. That's when I learned that estrogen HRT—prescribed for menopause—is made from hormones extracted from the urine of pregnant horses. I was horrified! Immediately, I threw away everything I had received from Dr. X— including the prescription I had just filled.

Not being one who likes taking pills of any kind, I never went back on any kind of estrogen HRT drugs. In addition, I found that after six months, I was no longer suffering from hot flashes with the exception of one or two a month. By the end of the year, I swear, I was hot flash free. Later, I researched "estrogens and menopause" and I've provided my findings herein.[33]

Since my surgeries, I have also suffered from numbness in my inner thigh on my left leg—up and through the left side of my labia. Although I am happy to report that even without my female parts, my sex drive has not diminished. Yet my orgasms were not the same without the feeling of the left side of my labia. Nor would normal intercourse be the same due to my bypass graft implant—pressure against my groin was now uncomfortable.

Although I returned to work nearly three months after the beginning of my medical absence, I would only remain working for my employer for four months more. During this period, I once again found time for my own endeavors. But my modified work schedule had taken its toll on my boss so I decided that it was best we said our goodbyes. It was perfect timing for my husband and I, since we had an upcoming cruise scheduled just three weeks away.

Unfortunately, due to my limitations directly caused by my botched hysterectomy, subsequent surgeries, coupled with my ongoing rehab, I was "derailed" from fundraising for our upcoming company. I needed my health back in order before I could pursue being CEO of my own company.

In addition, although our cruise through the Panama Canal was to serve both business purposes and personal purposes, I was "derailed" from the business purpose photoshoots. The good news was that we were able to shoot more than one-thousand photos to use in our fashion and style collections. However, due to my health limitations, we had to cancel all of our planned excursions off ship as I was still not able to walk distances because of my lack of endurance. Still in a lot of pain, I retired most nights early with a Percocet cocktail.

Walking continued to be problematic as I continued to suffer from constant pain in my leg. Nonetheless, I was fortunate to have a high tolerance for pain and was able to manage with the occasional

Percocet—instead of one every four hours. By the end of the first year, I was not able to walk more than a couple of short blocks without assistance. Typically, as I walked, the severity of my pain would grow until it would finally debilitate me and I'd have to stop.

One evening, however, I decided to challenge myself and walk several blocks to one of our favorite local hangouts—something we had always done before. At this particular hang out, my dad and his friends gathered once a week; and lately I had been the topic of conversation—so they were all anxious to see me. My husband and I slowly set out to make the journey. I made it, but I was in pretty bad shape afterwards—we had to take a cab home.

By the end of the year, I had an entirely new team of doctors through my husband's HMO. My doctor for internal medicine had worked with me to manage my pain. At one point, she issued me a handicap placard to assist with my walking limitations. But given the type of cars we drove and my youth, I received too much public flack that spurred retaliation. So I gave up the handicap placard. I've also stopped taking Percocet—she placed me on Ibuprofen to help with the pain and swelling when my leg worsened.

In addition to regularly scheduled mammograms, I also have a new OB/GYN, and a new vascular surgeon who placed me on annual surveillance to monitor my vascular graft. He was very thorough, sending me to a neurologist for a complete MRI—to make sure that my leg pain was directly related to blood flow and not any spinal or neurological disorders. My neurologist confirmed that I have nerve damage in my leg—where the suture was—and my injuries are solely due to my botched hysterectomy.

In addition, my doctor referred me to a dermatologist due to numerous scars and other marks left after the surgeries. I also asked her to review and monitor the size and shape of a birthmark on my hip going forward. Ongoing, I will see each of these doctors on an annual basis for continued care.

Second Year

31

During my second year, I experienced nominal changes in my recovery. Still suffering from chronic pain in my left foot and leg, and numbness in my thigh, I have learned how to manage both—rarely indulging in pain medication. Yet more frustrating, my husband and I have drastically modified our lifestyle to regain the joys in life we shared. Finally, at the end of the year, I had powered through my health issues—accepting my limitations—and began fundraising activities for our company.

Early in the year, we decided to move to better accommodate my limitations. We purchased a loft in a residential, shopping, dining, and entertainment district built around a main street called Santana Row in San Jose, California. At build out, this project covers an eighteen-block area and encompasses 680,000 square feet of restaurants and retail space (Burberry, Gucci, Ferragamo, and the likes), 1,201 residential units (lofts, flats, townhomes, and villas), a luxury hotel, ten spas and salons, movie theaters, art galleries, nightlife, and parks. The size and scope of this project made it one of the nation's largest mixed-use projects constructed by a single developer—it seemed more cohesive to our limited lifestyle.

After purchasing our new home (loft), my husband further indulged me and gave me thousands of dollars to remodel as I saw fit before moving in. This would allow me to put back on my interior design hat. Nevertheless, even with these modifications, I continue to have trouble walking to and from our surroundings without the help of holding my husband's hand.

With our new loft, we have an eighteen-step staircase leading to our primary bedroom—and my studio added by the remodel. We considered installing an elevator, but decided against it for space reasons. Over time, I learned that the more I used my leg—slowly going up and down the stairs—it felt like my foot and leg were improving; and at the same time, I noticed I was experiencing less pain.

Nonetheless, a few months later, I felt a new soreness in my leg as if something from the middle of my shin had dislodged and dropped to the bottom of my foot. Thereafter, when I walked downstairs, I felt a sharp stabbing at the bottom of my foot. Whatever it is, it feels like it is mobile. But from the outside of my foot I am not able to feel anything that might be inside. I wonder if maybe Dr. TooCool's broken surgical tool piece is still in my foot.

I reported my new symptom to my doctor and she referred me to a podiatrist. After a short visit, the podiatrist scheduled an MRI for the bottom of my foot. Discouraged, I found the MRI technician obnoxious and not helpful at all. She asked me to place a sticker at the position where I felt the sharp pain. Given my condition, it was difficult for me to bend down and reach the bottom of my foot and the technician refused to help—so I did my best under my circumstances. Of course nothing showed up on the MRI—she had only taken a couple of pictures and never even asked me to reposition my foot for a better view.

Perturbed by my new symptom and always the same outcome; there really was not much the doctors could do about anything it seemed. The damages caused by my botched hysterectomy were done—and permanent. So I decided to ignore whatever is in my foot, at least for the time being.

At the end of the year, my husband and I moved forward with fundraising activities for the launch of our new fashion and luxury goods company. We booked space in the hotel downstairs and held an exclusive night of entertainment followed by a business presentation—Series A Preferred Stock fundraising.

Guests included a combination of proposed stakeholders, partners, clients, family, and friends. Beverages were served, while our collections were being previewed, followed by a formal presentation announcing our story to the world—all at the same time. Following the presentation was an after party—sectioned off in the hotel bar where we hosted wine and hors d'oeuvres.

But for my botched hysterectomy and surprise find of endometriosis—during a time when the economy was booming prior to the current 2008 meltdown—I feel that securing funding would have easily been achievable. Instead, we'd now need to regroup . . .

Beyond

32

Amazingly, after my second year, I started to notice some improvement. I was now experiencing more good days than bad days—with the exception of the new pain at the bottom of my foot, which felt like a mobile object stabbing me. Although walking continued to bother me and continued to cause pain in my leg, I noticed that my lung capacity was stronger and walking no longer felt exhausting. As long as I masked the pain in my leg and foot, I was now able to walk much further. As well, the numbness in my thigh area and labia was almost gone by the middle of my third year.

Early on in the year, after making the decision to self-fund our company by pre-launching the publishing division—Aauvi House Publishing Group—I took on a new activity with my son. This would be the first book of a series of books titled, "Cooking with Mom: A Pre-Culinary Journey, Volume I—Herbs, Spices, and Cooking Techniques" that our publishing division was set to publish. "Cooking with Mom" is a voice and tone personality driven interview format between mom and son. Tip boxes with culinary terms of art, cooking techniques, and nutritional facts are within each recipe. Cook through cookbook in 4-weeks eating breakfast, lunch, snacks, dinner, and dessert while consuming approximately 1500 calories per day at a cost of less than $50.00 per week per person; complete with 4-week menu plans and accompanying grocery lists.

The constant physical movement of getting up and down from my computer—cooking, shopping, and researching—was improving the pain I had been experiencing in my leg. I also noticed that the pain in my foot seemed like it too had subsided. For a while it felt as if the object in my foot had taken up residence and a callous was forming around the object—but at least I rarely felt the sharp pain anymore.

More medical mysteries would ensue during my third year. After my annual surveillance ultrasound with my vascular surgeon, the findings indicated the implant was already showing signs of narrowing and plaque buildup. I realized that not only was Dr. TooCool's estimate on the lifespan of my graft wrong, but that my later internet findings proved accurate—indicating perhaps a much different lifespan than the five years that I was told—before more surgery!

Even more frightening was an episode I had with what seemed at the time to be a heart attack. I had been experiencing lightheadedness and difficulty breathing for a couple of weeks. I initially felt my symptoms were brought on by stress or lack of food intake. But the last spell included sweating and I felt like I was going to pass out. This prompted me to immediately call and schedule an appointment with my doctor. However, instead of setting up an appointment they transferred me to the hospital's advice nurse.

While I was on hold with the advice nurse, my landline phone was ringing. When I picked it up, it was my doctor. I guess the advice nurse had notified her about my condition.

After explaining my symptoms to my doctor, she wanted to call for an ambulance. I asked her not to as I wanted my husband to take me if I needed to go to the hospital. She reluctantly agreed, but only if I stayed on the phone with her until my husband arrived.

So with my doctor on the phone, I called my husband from my cell phone and told him I needed to get to emergency. He told me he was on his way home. Then I reported his whereabouts to my doctor.

As she continued questioning me, I was having a hard time standing. She wanted me to lie on the couch so that I wouldn't fall. But I told her that lying down made it difficult for me to breathe, and that I was more secure sitting. She agreed so I sat until my husband arrived.

After my husband arrived, I told my doctor and we quickly hung up. He walked me to our car and off we went to the emergency room. Again I was scared. I wondered if my previous surgeries had actually weakened my heart. Then, my husband scared too, started asking me questions causing me more anxiety. So I asked him to stop talking.

When we arrived at emergency I was immediately admitted. My heart rate was rapid and they didn't know why. I did what I had committed to do and had my husband call my parents and each of my sons—full disclosure. He would ask everyone to meet us at the hospital.

Shockingly, the emergency room doctor didn't seem to want to be bothered with me. After an hour had gone by and no one telling me anything, I requested to speak to her. She told me that she could find nothing wrong with me other than an accelerated heart rate. But because of my accelerated heart rate they had to be thorough. I would have to undergo a stress test in the morning, while they monitored my heart via an electro cardiogram. Meanwhile, I would be kept overnight—in emergency—while they continued to monitor my heart.

I then proceeded to tell her that I was starving—I hadn't eaten all day. I could tell she could care less, so I pressed and asked if my condition could be due to lack of nutrients. If so, I simply wanted to know if it was okay if I ate. Then she got smart with me—telling me the hospital wasn't a restaurant. I tried to explain that the only reason I was asking about food was so that I could ask my husband to go out and get some for me—I wanted to know if there was anything she didn't want me to eat. Instead, she told me to do whatever I wanted. Then she got smart with me again and said she had other patients that needed her and she needed to "go save lives." What a bitch I thought.

Of course my wonderful husband went out to get me food—a cheeseburger and chocolate shake from In-N-Out. After my meal, I told my family that they should go home and that I would be fine. Throughout the night, again, I had many conversations with God. I also was cautious and tried to stay calm as it was still difficult to breathe. I was finally able to fall asleep.

At around 2:00 a.m., I woke up feeling oddly rested. It felt as though something had passed through my system and I was fine now. Just then a male nurse appeared at my bedside. He told me that he was happy to see that my heart rate was no longer racing. I thanked him.

Soon after, another nurse came in, and she told me something unnerving. She explained that the majority of patients seen in emergency were there due to heart related problems. Yet most of the time, patients are later released and the root cause never found.

Later that morning, I would undergo the stress test. However, due to my leg limitations, they would do my electro cardiogram test via an intravenous feed. I handled the test easily. The doctor administering the test informed me that my heart could be compared to that of a twenty year old—I was thrilled. It seemed as though, even after all I had been through, my heart and lungs were in great shape.

Since my visit to the emergency room, I continue to manage my stress level; using common sense instead of the stress management classes my doctor had wanted me to attend. Although I was told stress wouldn't necessarily kill me, I know stress is not good for you either. I also wondered if maybe something actually did pass while I was in emergency that night—a blood clot perhaps. I will never know.

Reflections

Reflecting back on my nightmare, I had many conversations with God. I'd asked for His strength to live and made many promises to Him in return. Now, a couple of years later, my nightmare still haunted me.

Then one morning, I woke up and headed for my computer. I just started writing—the title came to me instantly. The more I wrote, the more I realized my story needed to be told. There are millions of women out there who knowingly or unknowingly are suffering from endometriosis.

My story was not just about a botched "routine hysterectomy." It was about a "routine hysterectomy" for fibroids and cyst that really was undiagnosed endometriosis.

Once my hysterectomy doctor opened me up, he was overwhelmed when he discovered that I had endometriosis. Yet he was an OB/GYN specialist. In his rush to do my "hysterectomy" he had to deal with my endometriosis first. In doing so, he over sutured me—went into areas he should never had been in—which began a chain reaction of nearly insurmountable problems.

Had I not had endometriosis, there is no doubt in my mind that my "routine hysterectomy" may have been performed flawlessly. I believe what moved me to start writing my story was God. He had, had many opportunities to take me anytime He wanted during my nightmare but didn't. I was allowed to live to tell my story and get the message out to other women. We need to take control of this disease instead of solely relying on doctors.

After researching what books had been written with respect to hysterectomies, fibroids, cysts, and endometriosis, I was surprised to learn that very few had been written by women for women—what women need to know.

Ironically, each ordeal in my personal story and research of medical facts thereafter, I found was filled with medical insights that women need to know. Even today, doctors admit that they know very little about endometriosis.

Again reflecting back, I realized I had several near death experiences throughout my nightmare. The first when I almost bled out after my initial surgery—blood pressure 80/20 and no one ordered blood on my behalf; however, clinically this was not a near death experience. Then two more brushes with death occurred before and again during my second surgery, when I stopped breathing and had to be resuscitated twice—clearly clinical near death experiences.

In addition, I nearly died from grossly infected wounds—staph infections; again, not a clinical near death experience. And then when I woke up in surgery; but did Dr. Oblivious almost overdose me to near death with his frantic reaction to put me back to sleep?

Throughout my nightmare and near-death experiences, I never saw any white lights. Moreover, according to this study, when my "lungs stopped working"—requiring a breathing tube—this clearly led to the beginning process of death. Yet, if I was beginning the process of dying during that period, I was not aware that I wasn't breathing, nor did I have any visions of white lights.

It could also be possible that when I woke up in surgery, I was one of the 10 to 20 percent of people who report lucid, well-structured thought processes, reasoning, memories, and sometimes-detailed recall of events during an encounter with death. On the other hand, it was documented that my anesthesia was changed and re-administered, which would support the notion I had awakened during surgery.

It could also be likely that during my various Post-Ops, when I was not aware of several reported conscious states, it was due to my having difficulty separating sleep from wakefulness and not any near-death experiences. I had reported, on several occasions, that it was very difficult to awake in various states of Post-Op. But this sounded more like symptoms associated with REM state of sleep while awake.[34]

Reflecting back even further, were their signs of pending death, days or even weeks before my initial surgery? I had known for quite some time that I was very ill, but doctor visits never provided any answers. I knew I was deteriorating and had no energy—I was tired all the time. I felt like I was dying but the doctors concluded otherwise. And then there was my premonition, my encounter with my deceased grandfather, or was it Jesus Himself?

Months after the dream, doctors would concur that I needed surgery. And then after my surgery, Dr. X seemed surprised that I was alive at all given the amount of endometriosis he had found in my body, which had escaped to my bladder and so on. He told us that had we waited much longer the endometriosis would have gotten into my blood stream and killed me. Was my dream possibly another brush with death? If I had accepted my grandfather or Jesus' gesture, would I have awakened from sleep or would I have died in my sleep?

Still reflecting back, after my nightmare was over, I would learn that my husband had been keeping a secret. Not only was he dealing with his wife and the possibility of losing her after a routine hysterectomy; but on the second day of my ordeal, he had received news that his father—after recently surviving brain surgery—had now been diagnosed with cancer of the lynphonodes and would require radiation and chemotherapy. I had always been my husband's rock, but he and my parents decided that my focus needed to be on my healing. And so, I was not told of his father's condition—my parents were there for him in my absence.

His father lived a few hours away, so his father's new wife would attend to him in my husband's absence—my husband is an only child. Incredibly, his father had again beaten all odds and survived the cancer as well as the treatments. His wife told us that dad's doctors had coined a phrase when referring to him, calling him "Ironman."

I was also told later that when his dad first called to tell my husband of his cancer, he would crack a joke after hearing about my ordeal: "I just wish God would get off the M's"—as we all had the same last name "Moeszinger."

Unfortunately, that would not be the case. Although I would survive and so would my husband's father, while on our cruise to the Panama Canal with my husband's father and step-mother, we learned that she had stage four cancer. God had not gotten off the "M's." She would live a mere six weeks after returning from our cruise—she was only fifty-six.

Reflecting back a little more I realized two things: First, it was the new symptom "frequent urination" that caused me to make another appointment to see my doctor. And on this visit I would listen to my instincts and follow what my body was trying to tell me. I pleaded with my doctor for the ultrasound and she finally agreed. It was this ultrasound, which prompted the call for a specialist, and ultimately a hysterectomy that would lead to the discovery of my endometriosis.

Secondly, but for Dr. X's botched surgery resulting in the internal bleeding and almost death, Dr. Lifesaver would not have come into the picture. Coincidentally, Dr. Lifesaver just happened to be an Oncologist specializing in female reconstructive surgery. He operated above the uterus. Had any other kind of doctor come to my rescue, I may not have received the vertical incision, which ultimately revealed the state of my bladder—my endometriosis had metastasized, moving outside of my reproductive organs. Assuming I lived through the hysterectomy, more than likely I would have required another surgery to remove the endometriosis from my bladder and have it repaired.

Although these revelations provided answers as to why I was seeing my doctor so often. Why didn't the ultrasound show that there were issues with my bladder? Or why didn't the doctor, who ultimately read the ultrasound images, find there were issues with my bladder? And why were they only concentrating on my supposed "fibroids and cyst?"

My newest symptoms were "frequent urination," doesn't that start at the bladder? One could reasonably assume that the ultrasound should have included pictures of my bladder as well, since I had voiced that symptom.

Reflecting back further yet, nearly three years ago, after my husband and I were first married. We reached out to my general practitioner to explore whether or not we'd be able to have children. My new husband was forty years old and had never had children of his own; so I felt it was my obligation to find out if we could have children together—in case this became an issue later in our marriage. So together we met with my doctor.

Initially she scheduled me for an ultrasound and he had to provide a semen specimen at a lab. Although I had had a tubal ligation after my third son, there were procedures available to reverse it. We were told that the ultrasound indicated that one of my tubes was healthy, but the other seemed like it had been "burned off." Yet my doctor was not alarmed by these findings and nothing more was said about it. Thereafter, my husband and I did not think anything of it at the time, as neither of us really wanted more children—we had my three sons.

Maybe I should have questioned my doctor more about the state of my tubes. Apparently, it was the scar tissue left by the endometriosis that had made my tube to look "burned off." So why hadn't she considered the possibility of endometriosis then? And more importantly, why didn't I question the situation? The incident had raised a red flag with my intuition but I dismissed it. Would her reaction have been different if she was an OB/GYN?

A general practitioner or GP is a medical practitioner who provides primary care and specializes in nothing and sees everything. A general practitioner treats acute and chronic illnesses and provides preventive care and health education for all ages and both sexes. They have particular skills in treating people with multiple health issues and co-morbidities.

Obstetrics and gynecology (often abbreviated to OB/GYN, OBG or O&G) are the two surgical specialties dealing with the female reproductive organs, and as such are often combined to form a single medical specialty and postgraduate training program. This combined training prepares the practicing OB/GYN to be adept at the surgical management of the entire scope of clinical pathology involving female reproductive organs, and to provide care for both pregnant and non-pregnant patients.

Dr. X was an OB/GYN and yet he did not diagnose the endometriosis or the urgency of an immediate hysterectomy—until he opened me up nearly four weeks later. One would think, with endometriosis being the number three disease affecting women—more than 9,000,000 women in the United States having diagnosed endometriosis and millions more outside of the United States—that an OB/GYN, such as Dr. X should have diagnosed my endometriosis. There are several procedures doctors can perform to diagnose endometriosis—so why aren't they? And why aren't they having these discussions with their female patients?

Sadly, I would later learn from my GP that she had referred another patient to Dr. X who suffered a similar result at the hands of Dr. X. Needless to say; she no longer refers patients to Dr. X.

Now that I think about it, nearly fifteen years ago, my ex-husband's German Sheppard—Siberian husky female mix—had fought endometriosis as well. I had come home after work one day and found

216

her very weak in a pool of blood. I immediately threw a camping tarp on the seat of our truck and lifted her into the truck—my husband was out of town. I rushed her to the veterinary clinic and was told she needed an immediate hysterectomy.

As typical of emergency situations, I was not able to get a hold of my husband at the time. So I made the decision to spend the money and have his dog undergo an emergency hysterectomy—$1,800 at the time. Her surgery was successful and she would be with us several more years.

Afterwards, the veterinarian told me that because we had never gotten her fixed, her female organs ravaged by endometriosis had grown to such a mass that they covered the bottom of a five-gallon barrel. I felt responsible having never gotten her fixed so I was happy with my decision—though my husband at the time thought otherwise.

Getting a dog or cat fixed means that they can no longer reproduce. In a male, the veterinarian removes the testicles in a procedure called neutering. In females, the ovaries and uterus are removed in a procedure called spaying (ovariohysterectomy). Getting your pet spayed or neutered not only prevents them from reproducing, it reduces urine odor, and eliminates a male dogs desire to mark his territory.

The moral of the story is, endometriosis is not limited to human females, but can be found in other female species as well. So why do so many of us take better care of our pets than we do ourselves? Why don't we take the time to understand our own basic anatomy? And why do we often leave such diagnoses up to our doctors to solely determine? Why are we not more involved? We should be!

Endometriosis

34

Were there other signs I should have paid attention to? Could I have prevented or at least minimized the worsening of my condition had I discovered my endometriosis sooner? Should I have gotten a second opinion early on? I knew I was not getting better. Should I have put my foot down earlier with my doctor?

What is endometriosis? Today, after a quick Google search on endometriosis, I learned just how ugly and common this disease is.[35]

I am shocked when I look back as I had all of these symptoms with the exception of bowel problems. Today, I read that symptoms of endometriosis: Pain before and during periods—yes, pain with sex; I was in such bad shape sex was a rare occurrence. Infertility—yes. Fatigue—chronic. Painful urination during periods—yes. Painful bowel movements during period as well as other gastrointestinal upsets such as diarrhea, constipation, nausea—yes. All of these.

Continuing my research on endometriosis, I find that diagnosis is considered uncertain until proven by laparoscopy. Laparoscopy is a minor surgical procedure done under anesthesia. A laparoscopy usually shows the location, size, and extent of the growths. This helps the doctor and patient make better treatment choices.

So, I ask, what causes endometriosis?

The cause of endometriosis is unknown. The retrograde menstruation theory (transtubal migration theory) suggests that during menstruation some of the menstrual tissue backs up through the fallopian tubes, implants in the abdomen, and grows. Some experts believe that all women experience some menstrual tissue backup and that an immune system problem or a hormonal problem allows this tissue to grow in the women who develop endometriosis.

Another theory suggests that endometrial tissue is distributed from the uterus to other parts of the body through the lymph system or through the blood system. A genetic theory suggests that it may be carried in the genes in certain families or that some families may have predisposing factors to endometriosis.

Surgical transplantation has also been cited in many cases where endometriosis is found in abdominal scars, although it has also been found in such scars when accidental implantation seems unlikely.

Another theory suggests that remnants of tissue from when the woman was an embryo may later develop into endometriosis, or that some adult tissues retain the ability they had in the embryo stage to transform reproductive tissue in certain circumstances.[36/37/38]

Well, some answers at least. My case would probably fall under the "retrograde menstruation theory," based on Dr. X's observations. After the first surgery he was surprised the endometriosis had not yet gone into my blood stream causing death. Moreover, the ultrasound tech's constant questioning, made sense based on the "surgical transplantation theory."

AFTERWORD

Originally, I wrote "Derailed: Memoirs of a Botched Hysterectomy—Hysterectomy to Remove Fibroids and Cyst Really was Endometriosis!" under the pseudo name Jaimi Taylor, out of a sincere desire to share my story with other women to shed light on a terrible disease too often undiagnosed—endometriosis which can lead to dire consequences.

But years later, I changed the title to: "When Death Knocked at My Door: The 5 Moments that Changed My Life" under my own name, Lori Ann Moeszinger, because it was the first-time in my life that I consciously realized the pattern and power of prayer. Regardless of my ordeal with a botched hysterectomy and bout with endometriosis, the more powerful message herein is the Secrets of Prayer . . . and how our powerful and merciful God responds to our prayers.

As you recall, throughout my terrifying journey through a seemingly endless comedy of errors, I mentioned over and over again my conversations with God. Prior to my fourth surgery, I even begged God, "I'll do anything you want if you please let me live to finish raising my two young boys." Not only did the Lord answer my prayers; looking further back in time, I realized He had always been there throughout my life preparing my way all along—God's calling for me to spread the word of Jesus Christ.

With that said, I have always been a bit of an information junky—it seemed more like an inborn deep passion of mine. I started my first publishing company, Step-by-Step Publications, a how-to book series with thirty-two titles; long before the Idiot's Guide series and Dummies series how-to books were developed. My first book, in 1994, I published "Starting Out—Step-by-Step Guide for Teens Succeeding in the '90s." My second book, in 1996, I published "Minor League—Step-by-Step Guide to Understanding Investment Basics." As well, I have written numerous books in between and ever since, some published and others in various states of writing.

But writing was not enough for me, I thought. I needed more. Then, in 1994, I also started my college journey: completing my associate's degree in 1996, my bachelor's degree in 1998, and my law degree in 2002. Since 2002, I have launched several companies, Aauvi Group, Inc., Aauvi House Publishing Group, Rags to Riches Entertainment, Fox House Publishing Group, Aauvicom Group, AuthorsOpen, among others—each brought on its own trials and successes. Through it all, I realized my true passion is in writing and teaching and not to run a fashion house and sell retail goods.

Unfortunately, it wouldn't be until 2016, when I surrendered to God that I'd hear God's calling loud and clear. That year—long overdue, I thought—I finally began my lifelong journey as a born-again Christian—answering God's Calling.

You can read more about this in my book, "Total Surrender: My Story and Your Blueprint to a Meaningful Life."

The 5 Moments that Changed My Life

In 2004, my marriage to my wonderful husband, Eric. Unbeknownst to me at the time, God blessed me with a provider for my family and me so that I could focus on God Himself.

In 2007, my covenant with God, when death knocked at my door, God answered my prayers and gave me more time on earth to finish raising my young sons before working for Him.

In 2016, my surrender to God after once again finding myself in complete despair. From that day forward, I have put God first in my life and started living the life God wanted for me—setting aside what I thought was best for myself. After doing so, more blessings were and continue to be abundant. I have never been happier!

In 2018, realizing we weren't building a home—for way too much money—on the lot we purchased in 2016 out of state in North Idaho. We were purchasing a home, two lots over, from our property; already built, larger lot size, more parking, much more private, and for the deal of the century! This is also the year I started working for God! God's will, not my will.

In 2021, the launch of The Ridge Publishing Group—answering God's call, spreading the Word of God in multiple new fresh ways. I'd found my true purpose in life as servant to others—researching, studying, teaching, writing, publishing, and marketing—in my walk with God.

Ever since 2016, over the last several years, I have focused on the knowledge of God and the study of the Bible. I have heard God's clarion call and this is what The Ridge Publishing Group and its imprint, Guardians of Biblical Truth is all about: focusing on God and the Bible while creating and designing new ways for learning, teaching and understanding in books, textbooks, documentaries in print, and board games and card decks.

At The Ridge Publishing Group and Guardians of Biblical Truth formats, our aim is to prepare and motivate people to live for eternity. We pray that this inspired message will bless you, and your family and friends. For more teaching like this, check out our online platforms listed at the end of this book.

Thank you. And may God bless you, dear readers.

APPENDIX
CAST OF CHARACTERS

First Hospital:

My Doctor: my general practitioner.

Dr. X: OB/GYN Specialist—general practitioner referral.

Dr. Miracle: first hospital, anesthesiologist.

Dr. Lifesaver: cancer doctor; female reconstructive surgeon.

Nurse-Godsend: Critical Care Unit primary nurse.

Dr. Y: head of the Critical Care Unit; also in law school.

Daughter Dearest: temporary personnel assigned to Critical Care Unit.

Hotlips: Doppler Lab technician.

Dr. Obnoxious: vascular surgeon; smitten with lab technician.

Second Hospital:

Dr. TooCool: vascular surgeon; performed two leg surgeries on me.

Nurse-Angel: my primary day nurse in the Progressive Care ward.

Nurse-Mother: head of the Progressive Care ward.

Dr. Oblivious: second hospital, anesthesiologist; I woke up in surgery.

Dr. Old: Dr. TooCool's colleague.

Nurse-Nightwatch: my primary evening nurse, Progressive Care ward.

Priest Pester: Catholic Priest at Catholic hospital.

Dr. Feelgood: Dr. Lifesaver's colleague.

Nurse-Ratched: weekend nurse.

Nurse-Yappy: substitute for Nurse-Angel; she had day off.
Wilson: my yellow happy face pillow
Dr. Z: urologist; Dr. TooCool referral.

ENDNOTES

Chapter 3 — First Brush with Death

Blood Pressure — Blood pressure is the force exerted by circulating blood on the walls of blood vessels and constitutes one of the principal vital signs of life, which also includes heartbeat, rate of breathing, and temperature. Blood pressure is generated by the heart pumping blood into the arteries and is regulated by the response by the arteries to the flow of blood.

An individual's blood pressure is expressed as systolic/diastolic blood pressure, for example, 120/80. The systolic blood pressure (the top number) represents the pressure in the arteries as the muscle of the heart contracts and pumps blood into them. The diastolic blood pressure (the bottom number) represents the pressure in the arteries as the muscle of the heart relaxes after it contracts. Blood pressure always is higher when the heart is pumping (squeezing) than when it is relaxing.

Systolic blood pressure for most healthy adults falls between 90 and 120 millimeters of mercury (mm Hg). Normal diastolic blood pressure falls between 60- and 80-mm Hg. Current guidelines define normal blood pressure as 120/80. Blood pressures over 130/80 are considered high.

Low blood pressure (hypotension) is pressure so low it causes symptoms or signs due to the low flow of blood through the arteries and veins. When the flow of blood is too low to deliver enough oxygen and nutrients to vital organs such as the brain, heart, and kidney, the organs do not function normally and may be permanently damaged.

[1] MedicineNet.com –

http://www.medicinenet.com/low_blood_pressure/article.htm

Blood Transfusions — There are risks associated with receiving a blood transfusion, and these must be balanced against the benefit which is expected. The most common adverse reaction to a blood transfusion is a *febrile non-hemolytic transfusion reaction*, which consists of a fever which resolves on its own and causes no lasting problems or side effects.

Hemolytic reactions include chills, headache, backache, dyspnea, cyanosis, chest pain, tachycardia, and hypotension.

Blood products can rarely be contaminated with bacteria; the risk of severe bacterial infection and sepsis is estimated, as of 2002, at about 1 in 50,000 platelet transfusions, and 1 in 500,000 red blood cell transfusions.

There is a risk that a given blood transfusion will transmit a viral infection to its recipient. As of 2006, the risk of acquiring hepatitis B via blood transfusion in the United States is about 1 in 250,000 units transfused, and the risk of acquiring HIV or hepatitis C in the U.S. via a blood transfusion is estimated at 1 in 2,000,000 (2 million) units transfused. These risks were much higher in the past before the advent of second and third generation tests for transfusion transmitted diseases. The implementation of Nucleic Acid Testing or "NAT" in the early 2000s has further reduced risks and confirmed viral infections by blood transfusion are extremely rare in the developed world.

[2] Wikipedia, the free encyclopedia –
http://en.wikipedia.org/wiki/Blood_transfusion

Chapter 4 — Welcome to My Nightmare

Cardiac Arrest — A cardiac arrest is different from (but may be caused by) a heart attack, where blood flow to the heart is interrupted. Arrested blood circulation prevents delivery of oxygen to the body. Lack of oxygen to the brain causes loss of consciousness, which then results in abnormal or absent breathing. Brain injury is likely if cardiac arrest goes untreated for more than five minutes. To improve survival and neurological recovery immediately treatment is important.

Cardiac arrest is a medical emergency that, in certain situations is potentially reversible if treated early. When unexpected cardiac arrest leads to death this is called sudden cardiac death. The treatment for cardiac arrest is cardiopulmonary resuscitation (CPR) to provide circulatory support, followed by defibrillation if a shockable rhythm is present. If a shockable rhythm is not present after CPR and other interventions, clinical death is inevitable.

[3] Wikipedia – http://en.wikipedia.org/wiki/Cardiac_arrest

Cardiopulmonary Resuscitation — CPR involves physical interventions to create artificial circulation through rhythmic pressing on the patient's chest to manually pump blood through the heart, called chest compressions, and usually also involves the rescuer exhaling into the patient (or using a device to simulate this) to inflate the lungs and pass oxygen into the blood, called artificial respiration. Some protocols now downplay the importance of the artificial respirations and focus on the chest compressions only.

CPR is unlikely to restart the heart; its main purpose is to maintain a flow of oxygenated blood to the brain and the heart, thereby delaying tissue death and extending the brief window of opportunity for a successful resuscitation without permanent brain damage. Advanced life support and defibrillation, the administration of an electric shock to the heart, is usually needed for the heart to restart. This only works for patients in certain heart rhythms, namely Ventricular Fibrillation (VF) or pulseless ventricular tachycardia, rather than the 'flat line' asystolic patient although CPR can help induce a shockable rhythm in an arrested patient.

CPR is generally continued, usually in the presence of advanced life support, until the patient regains a heartbeat (called "return of spontaneous circulation" or "ROSC") or is declared dead.

Used alone, CPR will result in few complete recoveries, and those who do survive often develop serious complications. Estimates vary, but many organizations stress that CPR does not "bring anyone back," it simply preserves the body for defibrillation and advanced life support. However, in the case of "non-shockable" rhythms such as Pulseless Electrical Activity (PEA), defibrillation is not indicated, and the importance of CPR rises. On average, only 5% - 10% of people who receive CPR survive. The purpose of CPR is not to "start" the heart, but rather to circulate oxygenated blood, and keep the brain alive until advanced care (especially defibrillation) can be initiated. As many of these patients may have a pulse that is impalpable by the layperson rescuer, the current consensus is to perform CPR on a patient who is not breathing.

WHEN DEATH KNOCKED AT MY DOOR

Studies have shown the importance of immediate CPR followed by defibrillation within 3 to 5 minutes of sudden VF cardiac arrest improves survival. In cities such as Seattle where CPR training is widespread and defibrillation by EMS personnel follows quickly, the survival rate is about 30%. In cities such as New York City, without those advantages, the survival rate is only 1% - 2%.

Type of Arrest	ROSC	Survival
Witnessed In-Hospital Cardiac Arrest	48%	22%
Un-Witnessed In-Hospital Cardiac Arrest	21%	1%
Bystander Cardiocerebral Resuscitation	40%	6%
Bystander Cardiopulmonary Resuscitation	40%	4%
No Bystander CPR (Ambulance CPR)	15%	2%
Defibrillation within 3 to 5 minutes	74%	30%

In most cases, there are a higher proportion of patients, who achieve a ROSC, where their heart starts to beat on its own again, than ultimately survive to be discharged from hospital (see table above). This is due to medical staff either being ultimately unable to address the cause of the arrhythmia or cardiac arrest, or in some instances due to other co-morbidities, due to the patient being gravely ill in more than one way.

Defibrillation is the definitive treatment for the life-threatening cardiac arrhythmias, ventricular fibrillation, and pulseless ventricular tachycardia. Defibrillation consists of delivering a therapeutic dose of electrical energy to the affected heart with a device called a defibrillator. This depolarizes a crucial mass of the heart muscle, terminates the arrhythmia, and allows normal sinus rhythm to be reestablished by the body's natural pacemaker, in the sinoatrial node of the heart.

Defibrillators can be external, transvenous, or implanted depending on the type used or needed. Some external units, known as automated external defibrillators (AEDs), automate the diagnosis of treatable rhythms, meaning that lay responders or bystanders are able to use them.

Manual external defibrillator units are used in conjunction with (or more often have inbuilt) electrocardiogram readers, which the healthcare provider uses to

230

diagnose a cardiac condition (most often fibrillation or tachycardia although there are some other rhythms which can be treated by different shocks). The healthcare provider will then decide what charge (in joules) to use, based on proven guidelines and experience, and will deliver the shock through paddles or pads on the patient's chest.

[4] Wikipedia – http://en.wikipedia.org/wiki/Cardiopulmonary_resuscitation

Advanced Life Support — ALS is a treatment consensus for cardiopulmonary resuscitation in cardiac arrest and related medical problems. It is practiced by in-hospital cardiac arrest teams, which generally consist of junior doctors from various specialties (anesthetics, general or internal medicine.)

ALS presumes that basic life supports (bag-mask administration of oxygen and chest compressions) are administered. The main algorithm of ALS, which is invoked when actual cardiac arrest has been established, relies on the monitoring of the electrical activity of the heart on a cardiac monitor. Depending on the type of cardiac arrhythmia, defibrillation is applied, and medication is administered. Oxygen is administered and endotracheal intubation may be attempted to secure the airway. At regular intervals, the effect of the treatment on the heart rhythm, as well as the presence of cardiac output, is assessed.

[5] Wikipedia – http://en.wikipedia.org/wki/Defibrillation

[6] Wikipedia – http://en.wikipedia.org/wiki/Advanced_life_support

Endotracheal Intubation — In medicine, intubation refers to the placement of a tube into an external or internal orifice of the body. Although the term can refer to endoscopic procedures, it is most often used to denote tracheal intubation. Tracheal intubation is the placement of a flexible plastic tube into the trachea to protect the patient's airway and provide a means of mechanical ventilation. The most common tracheal intubation is orotracheal intubation where, with the assistance of a laryngoscope, an endotracheal tube is passed through the mouth, larynx, and vocal cords, into the trachea. A bulb is then inflated near the distal tip of the tube to help secure it in place and protect the airway from blood, vomit, and secretions. Another possibility is nasotracheal intubation where a tube is passed through the nose, larynx, vocal cords, and trachea. Extubation is the removal of the tube.

Tracheal intubation is potentially a very dangerous invasive procedure that requires a great deal of clinical experience to master. When performed improperly (e.g., unrecognized esophageal intubation), the associated complications may rapidly lead to the patient's death. Consequently, tracheal intubation's role as the "gold standard" of advanced airway maintenance was downplayed (in favor of more basic techniques like bag-valve-mask ventilation) by the American Heart Association's Guidelines for Cardiopulmonary Resuscitation in 2000, and again in 2005.

[7] Wikipedia – http://en.wikipedia.org/wiki/Endotracheal_intubation

Jackson-Pratt Drain — A Jackson-Pratt drain, JP drain, or Bulb drain, is a surgical drainage device used to pull excess fluid from the body by constant suction. The device consists of a flexible rubbery bulb – shaped something like a hand grenade – that connects to an internal drainage tube. Removing the bulb's plug, squeezing air out of the bulb, and replacing the plug creates suction in the drainage tubing. Another method involves folding the drain in half while it is uncapped, then while folded, recapping the drain.

This action causes fluid to be gradually sucked out of the body and into the bulb itself. The bulb may be repeatedly opened to remove the collected fluid and squeezed again to restore suction. It is best to empty drains before they are more than half full to avoid the discomfort of the weight of the drain pulling on the internal tubing.

Patients or caretakers can "strip" the drains by taking a damp towel or piece of cloth and bracing the portion of the tubing closest to the body with their fingers, run the cloth down the length of the tube to the drain bulb. One can also put a little bit of lotion or mineral oil on their fingertips to lubricate the tube to make stripping easier. The portion of the tube closest to the exit point of the drain from the body should be gripped first, and once the length of the drain is stripped, the end closest to the bulb should then be released. This increases the level of suction and helps to move clots through the drainage tube into the bulb.

[8] Jackson-Pratt drain from Wikipedia, the free encyclopedia

http://en.wikipedia.org/wiki/Jackson-Pratt_drain

Ativan — Brand name "Ativan," generic name "Lorazepam," is a drug used for treating anxiety. It is in the benzodiazepine family, the same family that includes diazepam (Valium), alprazolam (Xanax), clonazepam (Klonopin), flurazepam

(Dalmane), and others. It is thought that excessive activity of nerves in the brain may cause anxiety and other psychological disorders. Gamma-aminobutyric acid (GABA) is a neutotransmitter, a chemical that nerves in the brain use to send messages to one another. GABA reduces the activity of nerves in the brain. Lorazepam and other benzodiazepines may act by enhancing the effects of GABA in the brain. Because lorazepam is removed from the blood more rapidly than many other benzodiazepines, there is less chance that lorazepam concentrations in blood will reach high levels and become toxic. Lorazepam also has fewer interactions with other medications than most of the other benzodiazepines. The FDA approved lorazepam in March 1999.

Lorazepam is used for the management of anxiety disorders, the short-term relief of symptoms of anxiety or anxiety associated with depression. The effectiveness of lorazepam and other benzodiazepines has not been adequately studied for treatment beyond four months. Lorazepam is effective for insomnia, panic attacks, and is used in combination with other medications to prevent nausea and vomiting resulting from chemotherapy. Lorazepam also is administered before anesthesia and used for prevention and treatment of alcohol withdrawal.

The most common side effects associated with lorazepam are sedation (15.9% of patients), dizziness (6.9% of patients), weakness, and unsteadiness. Other side effects include a feeling of depression, loss of orientation, headache, and sleep disturbance.

Like all benzodiazepines, lorazepam can cause physical dependence. Suddenly stopping therapy after a few months of daily therapy may be associated with a feeling of loss of self-worth, agitation, and insomnia. If lorazepam is taken continuously for longer than a few months, stopping therapy suddenly may produce seizures, tremors, muscle cramping, vomiting, and sweating.

[9] MedicineNet.com – http://www.medicinenet.com/lorazepam/article.htm

Chapter 5 — Hot Blooded

Sequential Compression Devices — Sequential Compression Devices or SCD's, (also known as Lymphodema pumps) are designed to limit the development of Deep Vein Thrombosis (DVT) and Peripheral Edema in immobile patients. When a patient is immobile for long periods of time, as in recuperation from an injury, blood tends to pool in the calf area of the lower leg. To combat this tendency, clinicians use the SCD. This consists of an air pump connected to a disposable sleeve by a series of air tubes. The sleeve is placed around the patient's leg. Air is then forced into different parts of the sleeve in sequence, creating pressure around the calves and improving venous return. Hospital units can utilize up to 10 sequential champers; most home units have three.

[10] Sequential Compression Devices

http://www.msdonline.com/biomed/meh/SCD.HTM

Chapter 7 — Blood Clots

American Academy of Family Physicians — It is the position of the American Academy of Family Physicians that 'hospital privileges' should be based on the individual physician's documented training and/or experience, demonstrated abilities and current competence. This general policy would of course apply to privileges in all areas. The Joint Commission and the American Medical Association hold similar positions. In this frame of reference, each doctor must establish such privileges at various hospitals in which they wish to practice or perform surgeries in.

[11] AAFP – http://www.aafp.org/online/en/home/practicemgt/

privileges/policystatements/hospitalprivileges.html

Deep Vein Thrombosis — Deep venous thrombosis (DVT) refers to a blood clot embedded in one of the major deep veins of the lower legs, thighs, or pelvis. A clot blocks blood circulation through these veins, which carry blood from the lower body back to the heart. The blockage can cause pain, swelling, or warmth in the affected leg.

Blood clots in the veins can cause inflammation (irritation) called thrombophlebitis. Severe complications of deep vein thrombosis occur when a clot breaks loose (or embolizes) and travels through the bloodstream, causing blockage of blood vessels (pulmonary arteries) in the lung. Called pulmonary embolism, this can lead to severe difficulty in breathing and even death, depending on the degree of blockage.

In the United States, about 2 million people per year develop deep vein thrombosis. Most of them are aged 40 years or older. Up to 600,000 are hospitalized each year for the condition.

Deep vein thrombosis can lead to a more serious complication, blood clots in the lung (pulmonary embolism). Statistics reveal that at least 650,000 patients die each year from pulmonary embolism, making it the third most common cause of death in the United States.

[12] Emedicinehealth – http://www.emedicinehealth.com/blood_clot_in_the_legs/article_em.htm

Peripheral Artery Disease — Your arteries carry blood rich in oxygen and nutrients from your heart to the rest of your body. When the arteries in your legs become blocked, your legs do not receive enough blood or oxygen, and you may have a condition called peripheral artery disease (PAD), sometimes called leg artery disease.

PAD can cause discomfort or pain when you walk. The pain can occur in your hips, buttocks, thighs, knees, shins, or upper feet. Leg artery disease is considered a type of peripheral arterial disease because it affects the arteries, blood vessels that carry blood away from your heart to your limbs. You are more likely to develop PAD as you age. One in 3 people aged 70 or older has PAD. Smoking or having diabetes increases your chances of developing the disease sooner.

The aorta is the largest artery in your body, and it carries blood pumped out of your heart to the rest of your body. Just beneath your belly button in your abdomen, the aorta splits into the two iliac arteries, which carry blood into each leg. When the iliac arteries reach your groin, they split again to become the femoral arteries. Many smaller arteries branch from your femoral arteries to take blood down to your toes.

Your arteries are normally smooth and unobstructed on the inside but, as you age, they can become blocked through a process called atherosclerosis, which means hardening of the arteries. As you age, a sticky substance called plaque can build up in the walls of your arteries. Plaque is made up of cholesterol, calcium, and fibrous tissue. As more plaque builds up, your arteries narrow and stiffen. Eventually, enough plaque builds up to reduce blood flow to your leg arteries. When this happens, your leg does not receive the oxygen it needs. Physicians call this leg artery disease. You may feel well and still have leg artery disease or sometimes similar blockages in other arteries, such as those leading to the heart or brain. It is important to treat this disease not only because it may place you at greater risk for limb loss but also for having a heart attack or stroke.

[13] VascularWeb – http://www.vascularweb.org/patients/NorthPoint/ Leg_Artery_Disease.html

Computerized Tomography Scan — 'CT scan' or Computerized Tomography scan, also known as, the CAT (computerized axial tomography) scan takes pictures of structures within the body created by a computer that takes the data from multiple X-ray images and turns them into pictures on a screen. The CT scan can reveal some soft-tissue and other structures that cannot even be seen in conventional X-rays. Using the same dosage of radiation as that of an ordinary X-ray machine, an entire slice of the body can be made visible with about 100 times more clarity with the CT scan.

The tomograms ("cuts") for CT are usually made 5 or 10 mm apart. The CT machine rotates 180 degrees around the patient's body. The machine sends out a thin X-ray beam at 160 different points. Crystals positioned at the opposite points of the beam pick up and record the absorption rates of the varying thicknesses of tissue and bone. The data are then relayed to a computer that turns the information into a 2-dimensional cross-sectional image.

[14] MedicineNet.com – http://www.medterms.com/script/main/ art.asp?articlekey=2878

Chapter 8 — Confessions

Changes in Electrolytes after Surgery — Electrolytes are needed to maintain the body's balance. The most common electrolytes replaced after surgery are magnesium, potassium, calcium, phosphate, and sodium. These are trace elements that are found in your blood and other body tissues. They help your body work. But they must be in balance with each other. Electrolytes are measured through lab blood tests.

- Magnesium is found in your body's cells. Over half is within your bones. It is vital to your metabolism and the workings of organs and neuromuscular tissue. It can be replaced through your diet. Sources of magnesium are dark green vegetables, whole grains, nuts, seeds, tap water, fruits, and meats. It can be replaced by giving oral or IV supplements. It must be run slowly by IV. It can take up to 24 hours to be absorbed.

- Potassium is vital to healthy heart function, cell growth, and muscle contraction. In your diet, good sources of potassium are dark green leafy vegetables, raisins, bananas, salt substitutes, and potatoes. While in the hospital, it can be replaced by giving oral or intravenous (IV) supplements. IV Potassium may cause pain at the IV site. Please let your nurse know if you have pain or burning when you receive it through an IV. Potassium pills or liquid may cause nausea if not taken with meals or a snack.

- Calcium helps with nerve impulses, cardiac function, blood clotting, forming teeth and bone, and helping muscles contract. Calcium works closely with phosphorus. It is found mostly in the bones. Food sources are dairy products, salmon, fortified fruit juices, and dark green leafy vegetables. It is most often replaced with oral supplements like calcium carbonate (TUMS®). In severe cases, it may be given through an IV.

- Phosphate helps with the function of muscle, red blood cells and the nervous system. With calcium, it assists in forming bone and teeth. It is absorbed in the small bowel. It can be found in milk, cheese, eggs, meat, fish, and nuts. Oral supplements may be used to treat mild phosphate loss. More severe lack of phosphate may be helped with IV supplements such as sodium phosphate or potassium phosphate.

- Sodium and water work hand in hand to maintain a proper fluid volume in the body. The kidneys respond to the amount of sodium. They will either conserve fluid or get rid of (excrete) it. Sodium helps control your blood pressure. IV fluids help control proper sodium levels.

The proper balance of fluids and electrolytes will aid in your recovery.

[15] UWHealth – http://www.uwhealth.org/healthfacts/B_Extranet_HEALTH_INFORMATION-FlexMember-Show_Public_HFFY_1126658729712.html

Chapter 10 — Summer Heat

Central Line — A central line is also called a central venous line or a central venous catheter (CVC). A central line is a tube that is passed through a vein to end up in the chest portion of the large vein returning blood to the heart or in the right atrium of the heart.

A central line allows concentrated solutions to be infused with less risk of complications. It permits monitoring of special blood pressures including the central venous pressure, the pulmonary artery pressure, and the pulmonary capillary wedge pressures. The central line can be used for estimation of cardiac output and vascular resistance. The near end of the tube may also be connected to a chamber for injections given over periods of months. A central line saves having to have frequent small injections or "drips" placed in the arms.

The possible complications of a central line include air in the chest due to a punctured lung, bleeding in the chest, fluid in the chest, bleeding into or under the skin and infection. If the line becomes disconnected, air may enter the bloodstream and cause problems with breathing or a stroke.

[16] MedicineNet.com – http://www.medterms.com/script/main/art. asp?articlekey=14394

Chapter 13 — No White Lights

Spinal, Epidural and General Anesthesia — *What is a Spinal anesthetic?* Spinal anesthesia is placed in the low back (lumbar region). After a sterile prep and draping, local anesthetic is placed in the skin to numb the area where the Spinal needle will be placed. The spinal needle passes between the vertebrae of the Spinal column through the Dural membrane where the cerebrospinal fluid is located. Once the placement of the needle is accomplished medicines including a local anesthetic and sometimes a narcotic are dispensed via the needle. The needle is then removed. The entire process usually takes anywhere from 5 to 20 minutes.

What is Epidural anesthesia? Epidural anesthesia is most commonly placed in the low back (lumbar region). Unlike Spinal this technique may also be accomplished in the mid-back (thoracic region) for surgery in the area of the chest. After a sterile prep and draping, local anesthetic is placed in the skin to numb the area where the Epidural needle will be placed. The needle for Epidural passes between the vertebrae of the Spinal column to the Epidural space. Once the position is verified, a very small catheter (tube) is placed via the needle. The needle is then removed, and the catheter remains in the Epidural space. The catheter is then taped to the patients back. Local anesthetics and narcotics are given epidurally via this catheter. The procedure usually takes 10 to 25 minutes.

Who administers the Spinal or Epidural anesthetic? An anesthesiologist is a physician who specializes in the treatment of pain and the methods used to make a patient unable to sense the pain associated with surgery. Anesthesiologists are fully trained physicians who have completed medical school plus an internship and 3 years of training in anesthesia. Most anesthesiologists are Board Certified or Board eligible by the American Board of Anesthesiology.

What is it like to have a Spinal or Epidural? Is it painful? In order to place the Spinal or Epidural the patient must have an IV in place. The patient is placed on various monitors (pulse oximeter, BP, EKG). The patient is then positioned in either the sitting or lateral position. Once the local anesthetic is placed on the skin there should be a pressure sensation when the Spinal or Epidural needles are placed. As these needles are being placed sometimes a patient may feel a strong tingling in the area of the hip or shooting down the leg. This is usually only a transient sensation and should not alarm the patient. The anesthesiologist should be informed of this. It is important for the patient to hold still during the procedure. Once the anesthetic has been placed the patient will begin to feel warming of the bottom and legs followed by loss of sensation of the involved area. This is followed by a loss of strength. The time period is anywhere from 5 to 25 minutes.

Is there a risk of being paralyzed or permanent damage? The risk of paralysis is extremely low. The actual incidence of neurologic dysfunction resulting from bleeding complications is estimated to be 1 in 150,000 for Epidurals and 1 in 220,000 for Spinal anesthetics.

What are the risks of Spinal and Epidural anesthesia? Post-Dural puncture headache occurs infrequently with these techniques. The risks are 1% with Epidurals and 3% with Spinals. This is believed to be due to a leak of cerebrospinal fluid from the needle hole in the Dura. The occurrence of this is greatly reduced by using a smaller needle when possible. If this headache does occur it may be treated initially with hydration and pain medicines. If the headache does not resolve it would be treated with an Epidural blood patch. This is essentially using the patient's own blood to block the leak via the Epidural technique.

Backache is an infrequent problem. It most likely is due to ligament strain due to profound muscle relaxation or surgical positioning.

Other complications that can occur include, but are not limited to, low blood pressure, infection, nerve damage (including paralysis, loss of bladder and bowel function, loss of sexual function), allergic reactions, seizures, cardiac arrest, and death. Although the results of these are severe, they occur very rarely.

Will I be awake during the surgery? The patient will usually be sedated via intravenous medications during the surgery and many times before placement of the Spinal or Epidural. It is possible to sedate the patient so that they will be comfortable and without anxiety during the surgical procedure. It is the understanding of the anesthesiologist that most patients do not want to know what is going on while surgery is being carried out. In fact, a lot of patients even may not remember receiving a Spinal or Epidural anesthetic.

Is Spinal or Epidural used along with general anesthesia? In surgery on the blood vessels, the chest and for post-operative pain control Spinal or Epidural may be used along with general anesthesia. There are some great benefits from these techniques which include decreased blood loss during surgery, decreased risks of phlebitis, and a reduced risk of stress reaction as a direct result of the patient having surgery.

In the case of Spinal, when narcotics are added, this can give a patient anywhere from 12 to 24 hours pain relief after surgery. Epidural is much longer pain control because a small catheter is placed in the back, and this may be used for 1 to 4 days post operatively.

[17] Redding Anesthesia Associates Medical Group – http://www.redding anesthesia.com/spinal.htm

Chapter 15 — Cover Up

White Blood Cell Count vs. Red — *What does the blood do?* The blood circulates throughout the body. It carries nutrients (food) and oxygen to all the cells of the body;

and carries away waste products so that they can be removed from the body. Without access to the blood, cells and body tissues die.

The blood moves around the body inside the circulatory system. This is made up of blood vessels (tubes) called arteries, veins and capillaries. The blood keeps moving through these blood vessels because it is pumped by the heart.

Arteries carry blood that is full of oxygen from the heart to all parts of the body. As the arteries get further and further away from the heart, they get smaller and smaller. Eventually they turn into capillaries. These are the smallest blood vessels. They go right into the tissues. Here the blood in the capillaries gives oxygen to the cells and picks up the waste gas, carbon dioxide, from the cells.

The capillaries are connected to the smallest veins in the body. The veins get bigger and bigger as they carry the blood back towards the heart. The blood passes through the right side of the heart and goes to the lungs where it gets rid of carbon dioxide and picks up more oxygen. It then passes through the left side of the heart and is pumped back around the body.

The blood always circulates through the body in the same direction. As well as oxygen and carbon dioxide, many other substances are carried in the blood. The blood circulating through the digestive system picks up digested food products and carries them to the liver to be used or stored.

The circulation can help explain why some cancers nearly always spread to the same place. Cancers of the colon (large bowel) often spread to the liver. This is because blood circulates from the bowel through the liver on its way back to the heart. If there is a cancer in the large bowel, and some cancer cells escape into the circulation, they may stick in the liver as the blood passes through. They can then begin to grow into secondary cancers.

What is in blood? Although blood looks like a red liquid, if some is left in a test tube it separates out into a pale liquid called plasma and a solid layer of blood cells. The blood is about 55% plasma and 45% cells. Plasma is mostly water with some proteins and other chemicals dissolved in it. There are three main types of cells in the blood: white blood cells, red blood cells, and platelets.

What are white blood cells? There are several different types of white cells in the blood in differing amounts. They all play a part in the immune response. This is the response of the body to infection, or anything else the body recognizes as 'foreign'. These blood cells can be made very quickly and generally have a short life. Some only live for a few hours, others for days.

There isn't an exact 'normal' figure for blood counts. 'Normal' for a large man wouldn't be the same as for a small woman. But generally, the normal white cell count is between about 4,000 and 11,000 per cubic millimeter of blood. If you have surgery or an infection, your white blood cell counts will go up within a day or two.

The most numerous of the white blood cells are the neutrophils. There are between 2,000 and 7,500 of these per cubic millimeter of blood. They are important for fighting infection. If you have chemotherapy, particularly in high doses, your neutrophil count usually drops quickly.

The next most numerous are the lymphocytes. A normal lymphocyte count is between 1,300 and 4,000 per cubic millimeter of blood. Lymphocytes are involved in making antibodies as part of the immune response.

Other white blood cells are present in smaller numbers in the circulating blood. These figures are taken from the Oxford Handbook of Clinical Medicine.

What are red blood cells? Red blood cells give the blood its red color. There are more than 4 or 5 million of them in every cubic millimeter of blood. A red blood cell can live for up to 120 days.

Red blood cells are able to attach to oxygen to carry it within the circulation to the tissues. When they get to an area where the oxygen is needed, they give it up and pick up carbon dioxide which they carry back to the lungs. A shortage of red blood cells is called anemia.

What are Platelets? Platelets are really bits of much bigger cells called megakoryocytes. A normal platelet count is between 150,000 and 440,000 per cubic millimeter of blood. Platelets are very important in blood clotting. They clump together to form a plug if bleeding occurs. Then they release other chemicals that help the blood to clot and the blood vessel to be repaired.

How and where are blood cells made? All the different types of blood cells develop from one type of cell called a 'blood stem cell'. In adults, blood stem cells are normally found in the red bone marrow inside the bones. Blood cells are made in the bone marrow in the skull, ribs, sternum (breastbone), spine and pelvis. The stem cells divide and multiply to make the blood cells. These cells differentiate (develop and mature) as they grow into white cells, red cells, or platelets. It is now possible to collect stem cells and freeze them.

[18] CancerHelp UK – http://www.cancerhelp.org.uk/about-cancer/what- is-cancer/body/the-blood-and-circulation

Chapter 16 — Dark Comedy of Errors

Heparin and Coumadin for DVT — Heparin and Coumadin (warfarin) are two types of blood thinners (anticoagulants) commonly used in deep vein thrombosis treatment. Though they're called blood thinners, these DVT treatments do not actually thin blood…but can keep existing blood clots from getting larger or prevent new ones from forming. They do this by preventing the production of certain proteins needed for blood to clot.

Heparin – Traditionally, people have received heparin intravenously (by IV into a vein) in the hospital for about 5 to 7 days. However, low-molecular-weight heparin is effective within hours, reducing complications and hospitalizations. You can give yourself the injections at home, once or twice daily, on an outpatient basis. And because low-molecular-weight heparin is more consistent and predictable, it doesn't require regular blood tests.

Coumadin – You take Coumadin by pill once a day, beginning while you're still on heparin. Treatment may continue for about 3 to 6 months. While on Coumadin, you need regular blood tests to ensure you have the correct dosage.

Monitoring your blood while on Coumadin for DVT is a balancing act. Coumadin decreases blood clotting. You want to receive enough Coumadin to decrease your risk for blood clots, but not so much that clotting stops completely. If this happens, you're at high risk for bleeding problems. This is why the doctor needs to monitor your blood…

The test used most often to monitor the effect of Coumadin is called prothrombin time (PT). The results of this test determine how high or low your dose of Coumadin should be. Your dose may be higher when you first begin treatment, then it may be adjusted to a maintenance level. The doctor may also adjust your Coumadin dose in response to your circumstances, such as being scheduled for surgery or needing to take other medications.

To prevent bleeding problems, take these precautions while you're on heparin and Coumadin: don't smoke; use a soft toothbrush; floss with waxed floss, instead of unwaxed floss; instead of a straight or blade razor, use an electric razor; wear gloves while gardening or doing other household projects; avoid rough sports, but wear protective gear for activities such as bicycling.

Foods that are rich in vitamin K can make Coumadin less effective. Try to avoid large amounts of these foods, but do not suddenly lower your intake without discussing this with your doctor: beef or pork liver; green tea; alfalfa; asparagus; broccoli; sprouts; cabbage; cauliflower; lettuce, spinach, kale or turnip greens; watercress; canola and soybean oil.

Also, talk with your doctor before taking vitamin E or changing your dose. Vitamin E may increase the impact of Coumadin. Avoid alcohol or drink only limited amounts. It can also impact how your body handles Coumadin.

Potential side effects of heparin and Coumadin include excessive bleeding; red or dark brown urine; red, dark brown, or black stool; periods that are heavier than usual; bleeding gums; nosebleeds; cuts that don't stop bleeding; severe headache or stomach pain or upset; weakness, faintness, or dizziness; frequent bruises or blood blisters; skin rash or irritation; unusual fever; joint or back pain; swelling or pain at an injection site.

[19] WebMD – http://www.webmd.com/dvt/dvt-treatment-tips-for- taking-heparin-and-warfarin-safely

Heparin and Coumadin for PAD — Peripheral Arterial Disease: Adding Coumadin to antiplatelet therapy only increases bleeding risk. The addition of anticoagulants to antiplatelet therapy does not improve outcomes in peripheral arterial disease and significantly increases the risk for life-threatening bleeding, according to a study in the current *New England Journal of Medicine*.

In the international WAVE trial, researchers randomized some 2,100 patients with peripheral arterial disease either to antiplatelet therapy alone or to combination therapy with antiocoagulants. After 35 months of follow-up, there were no significant differences between the groups in MI, stroke, severe peripheral or coronary ischemia, or death from cardiovascular causes.

Life-threatening bleeding, and in fact bleeding of any severity, was significantly higher with combination therapy.

Writing in *Journal Watch General Medicine*, Allan S. Brett comments that although combination therapy in peripheral arterial disease is no longer in general use, "patients with PAD sometimes receive Coumadin for other reasons and are continued on that drug even after the non-PAD indication disappears; this study strongly suggests that patients would be better off taking aspirin alone."

[20] JournalWatch Physician's First Watch – http://firstwatch.jwatch. org/cgi/content/full/2007/719/1

Chapter 17 — Singing Bear Telegram

AirLife Volumetric Incentive Spirometer — An Incentive Spirometer is a type of medical equipment used to help patients improve the functioning of their lungs. The AirLife Volumetric Incentive Spirometer is ideal for patients who have had any surgery that might jeopardize functioning of the lungs. Patients who have had lung surgery, heart surgery or other surgeries involving extended periods of time under anesthesia with a lot of in-bed recovery time commonly use an Incentive Spirometer.

The patient breathes in from the AirLife Volumetric Incentive Spirometer as slowly and as deeply as possible. An indicator provides a gauge of how well the patient's lung or lungs are functioning. The patient is generally asked to do many repetitions a day while measuring his or her progress by way of the gauge on the AirLife Volumetric Incentive Spirometer.

Volumetric Incentive Spirometers help simplify deep breathing therapy, using features that prompt patients to perform and monitor their own postsurgical breathing exercises. An adjustable goal indicator provides a volumetric guideline for adequate lung exercise with Incentive Spirometer. Dual-sided calibrations allow clear, legible identification of volumes. The inspiratory indicator encourages patients to maintain an appropriate rate of inspiration. The AirLife Volumetric Incentive Spirometer is constructed of sturdy plastic and is compact for convenient use and storage.

[21] ActiveForever.com – http://www.activeforever.com/p-1746-volumetric-incentive-spirometer-by-airlife.aspx

Chapter 19 — Dire Straits

Blood in the Urine Implications — Blood in the urine is a common problem. The medical term for red blood cells in the urine is hematuria. Sometimes blood in the urine is a sign of serious problem in the urinary tract, while other times it is not serious and requires no treatment. Only after a thorough evaluation by a healthcare provider should blood in the urine be attributed to a non-serious cause.

The urinary tract consists of the following structures:

- Kidneys: You have two kidneys, located closer to your back than your front at about waist level. The kidneys filter the blood in your body and produce urine.
- Ureters: These narrow, hollow tubes carry urine from the kidneys to the bladder.
- Bladder: The bladder is a balloon-like organ that holds urine until it is convenient for you to empty your bladder (urinate).
- Urethra: This narrow, hollow tube carries urine from the bladder to the outside of your body. The flow of urine is controlled by internal and external sphincter muscles, which tighten or relax around the urethra, holding or releasing urine.

Blood in the urine is not always visible. If the amount of blood is small, the urine can look normal. This is called microscopic hematuria because the blood cells are visible only under a microscope. Typically, this is discovered when the patient has a urine test for some other reason.

When there is enough blood to be visible, the urine may look pinkish, red, or smoky brown (like tea or cola). This is called gross or frank hematuria. It takes very little blood in urine to be visible – about 1/5 of a teaspoon in a half quart of urine.

A trace amount of blood in your urine is normal. The average person with a healthy urinary tract excretes about 1 million red blood cells (RBC) in the urine each day. This amount of blood is not visible. This is not considered to be hematuria.

An abnormal amount of blood in the urine can be acute (new, occurring suddenly) or chronic (ongoing, long term). Acute hematuria can occur just once, or it can occur many times.

Sometimes the urine can appear with a color indicating hematuria though the urine actually does not contain red blood cells, but rather is discolored by medications or foods. This can be distinguished by a urinalysis (UA) test.

Up to 10% of people have hematuria. About 3% of people develop gross hematuria. Women develop hematuria more than men because women are more likely to have urinary tract infections. Older adults, especially men, have hematuria more often than younger people because they are more likely to take medications that can irritate the urinary tract, have enlargement of the prostrate, or cancer.

What causes blood in the urine? Hematuria has many different causes. Blood in the urine can come from any condition that results in infection, inflammation, or injury to the urinary system. Typically, microscopic hematuria indicates damage to the upper urinary tract (kidneys), while visible blood indicates damage to the lower tract (ureters, bladder, or urethra).

But this is not always the case. The most common causes in people younger than 40 years of age are kidney stones or urinary tract infections. These may also cause hematuria in older people, but cancers of the kidney, bladder, and prostate become a more common concern in people older than 40 years of age.

Several conditions causing hematuria may exist at the same time. Some causes of hematuria are serious, others are not. Your healthcare provider will perform tests to help tell the difference.

The well-known causes of blood in the urine include: kidney stones; infections of the urinary tract (UTIs) or genitals; blockage of the urinary tract, usually the urethra: by a stone, a tumor, a narrowing of the opening (stricture), or a compression from surrounding structures; cancer of the kidney, bladder, or prostate; kidney disease; blood clotting disorders; injury to the upper or lower urinary tract, as in a car accident or a bad fall; medications: antibiotics (Rifadin), analgesics such as aspirin, anticoagulants (blood thinners such as Coumadin), and others.

Sometimes no cause is found for blood in the urine. If serious conditions such as cancer, kidney disease, and other chronic diseases that cause kidney damage or bleeding are ruled out, the cause is usually not serious. The hematuria will probably go away by itself or continue as a chronic condition without doing harm. Any changes should immediately trigger a return visit and evaluation by your healthcare provider.

The prognosis depends on the cause of the bleeding. The prognosis for most people is good, because the most common causes of blood in the urine can be cured. People who are otherwise healthy can usually be treated on an outpatient basis.

[22] Emedicinehealth – http://www.emedicinehealth.com/blood_in_the_urine/article_em.htm

Chapter 20 — Stabilized

Endometriosis — Endometriosis is one of the most common gynecological conditions in the United States. We don't know exactly how many American women suffer from this disease, but best estimates set the number at about 5 million. Women of all ages, races and backgrounds have been found to have endometriosis. Recent information suggests that the disease is becoming more prevalent. Some 2 million women had hysterectomies for pelvic pain related to endometriosis between 1965 and 1984. Over that time period, the number of hysterectomies performed per year for this condition doubled. In addition, the proportion of all hysterectomies performed because of endometriosis rose from approximately 10% to 20%.

[23] A Gynecologist's Second Opinion – http://www.gynsecondopinion.Com/endometriosis.htm

Endometriosis and Scar Tissue — Endometriosis is a disorder of the female reproductive system. In endometriosis, the endometrium, which normally lines your uterus, grows in other places as well. Most often, this growth is on your fallopian tubes, ovaries or the tissue lining your pelvis.

When endometrial tissue is located elsewhere in your body, it continues to act as it normally would during a menstrual cycle: it thickens, breaks down and bleeds each month. Because there's nowhere for the blood from this displaced tissue to exit your body, it becomes trapped, and surrounding tissue can become irritated.

Trapped blood may lead to cysts, scar tissue and adhesions – abnormal tissue that binds organs together. This process can cause pelvic pain, especially during your period. Endometriosis also can cause fertility problems.

[24] MayoClinic.com – http://www.mayoclinic.com/health/endometrio sis/ds00289

Fibroids and Cysts — Uterine fibroids, also known as fibroid tumors, are benign (noncancerous) growths on the uterus. Uterine fibroids occur in 20 to 40 percent of all women older than 35 years of age.

Uterine fibroids are rubbery nodules that begin as irregular cells in the muscular layers of the uterus and grow slowly into tumor-like masses of connective tissue and smooth muscle.

Uterine fibroids may be as small as a pea or the size of a basketball. A woman can have one or many uterine fibroids. The growth of uterine fibroids is unpredictable. They may remain relatively stable, or they may increase in size rapidly. Rarely do uterine fibroids become cancerous (less than 0.1 percent).

Uterine fibroids are unlikely to shrink or disappear on their own until after menopause. After menopause, no new uterine fibroids are likely to develop, and those already present usually shrink in size.

[25] Health Encyclopedia – Diseases and Conditions
http://www.healthscout.com/ency/68/148/main.html

Fibroids and Cysts — Ovarian cysts are filled with fluid, similar to a blister. They are located on/in the ovary, which is an organ that produces a follicle (egg) every month for the ovulation and menstrual cycles. The two ovaries are located on the left and the right of the uterus.

Ovarian cysts are very common, particularly in women between the ages of 30 and 60. Most are benign (noncancerous), but approximately 15 percent are malignant (cancerous). There are five common types of ovarian cysts: functional cysts, polycystic ovaries, endometrial cysts, cystadenomas, and dermoid cysts.

[26] Hope for Fibroids – http://www.hopeforfibroids.org/pictures.html

Chapter 22 — Bypass Graft Implant

Arterial Femoro-Femoral Bypass Graft — *Why did I need an operation to improve the blood supply to my leg?* The majority of patients with hardening of the arteries in the legs do not require surgery. Most patients have a degree of disability which is manageable by adjustments in lifestyle. Treating vascular risk factors reduces the risk of further problems due to atherosclerosis.

Hardening of the arteries in the legs only leads to serious problems in a small number of patients. However, if hardening of the arteries progresses, then there may be a risk of amputation.

Arterial bypass surgery is indicated in patients with a threatened leg likely to require amputation, if left untreated (critical limb ischaemia). It can also be considered in patients with very severe disabling claudication. Arterial bypass surgery can save the leg or reverse severe disability. The benefits of bypass surgery in patients with lifestyle limiting claudication are more controversial. Many surgeons will advise against such surgery in these circumstances as surgery may precipitate problems as well as solve them.

Arterial bypass surgery is not minor surgery. Operations are frequently prolonged, complex and carry significant risks. A decision to proceed with an operation to improve the blood supply to a leg needs to be taken in a careful and considered way. It will be the right option for many patients. In other patients an amputation may be more appropriate. In some very sick patients, nearing the end of their lives, the compassionate option may be to avoid any type of treatment and allow the patient to die peacefully.

How will I know if my leg is in danger? It is usually clear when the leg is in danger. Most patients will experience at least one of the following symptoms:

- **Rest pain** – This is a severe, continuous pain felt in the toes and foot. Some patients find that they only experience this pain at night. This is because during the day when the leg is down, gravity can assist the flow of blood. When the leg is elevated at night this gravity assistance disappears. Many patients find that dangling the foot over the edge of the bed can help to ease the pain. The pain is often very severe, and patients will sleep in a chair to avoid the discomfort of elevating the leg.

- **Gangrene** – If the blood supply deteriorates to a stage where insufficient blood is available to keep the tissues alive then gangrene can develop. This means that the tissue has died and turns black. If the tissues remain dry (mummified) then sometimes a toe can auto amputate and drop off without surgery. If it becomes wet (infected) then surgery is frequently required.

- **Ulceration and loss of tissue** – Sometimes frank gangrene does not develop but the tissues can ulcerate. In this situation the superficial tissues die and are shed leaving an ulcer crater which will not heal because the blood supply is so poor.

- **Severe disabling claudication** – Some patients experience none of the above symptoms, but they can develop claudication symptoms after a few steps and managing a normal life becomes virtually impossible.

What will happen if I do not have an operation? Amputation is the most likely outcome in patients with critical limb ischaemia (ulceration, gangrene, rest pain), who do not have bypass surgery to improve the blood supply to the leg. In patients with critical limb ischaemia, ulceration and gangrene will not resolve without some form of intervention. Improving the blood supply to the leg can allow healing to take place, but the gangrenous areas still need removal to enable healing to take place.

In patients with severe claudication, but no features of critical ischaemia, prediction of outcome can be difficult. Most surgeons would accept that bypass surgery is reasonable in these circumstances, if walking is becoming impossible even in the absence of gangrene, ulceration, or rest pain. Without surgery amputation is not inevitable. Many patients with severe claudication will merely continue with their symptoms and they may not deteriorate.

It must be acknowledged that there are patients in whom amputation may be the most appropriate way forward. There are many reasons for this, but the potential benefits of the operation for any individual must always be balanced against the potential risks and complications.

How do bypass operations work? The essential problem in all patients undergoing bypass surgery to the lower legs is that insufficient blood and hence oxygen is able to reach the tissues of the leg and foot. The tissues are starved of oxygen, and this is what leads to pain, gangrene, and ulceration.

Bypass operations work by improving the blood supply and hence the oxygen supply to the tissues that have been starved of oxygen. To do this the surgeon must take blood from a good artery above the area where the artery is blocked and take the blood along a tube (the conduit) to a good artery below the blocked segments.

There are variations on this principle when blood can be taken from one side of the body to the other (femoro-femoral crossover) or blood is diverted from arteries to the arms down to the legs (axillo-bifemoral grafting).

251

What operation will be performed? Inflow operations are performed to restore blood flow to the top of the leg. When the blood flow is normal to the legs, femoral pulses can be felt around the groin area. If major blood vessels (aorta or iliac arteries) are blocked, then the blood flowing into the leg is severely reduced. An inflow operation is required to restore this flow to normal.

There are many operations to restore inflow to the legs, but the following was on-point with respect to my operation by Dr. TooCool:

- **Femoro-femoral cross-over grafting** – These grafts originate from a normal femoral artery in the groin on one leg and take blood to the femoral artery in the groin on the opposite leg. For example, a graft is running from the left femoral artery in the patient to the right femoral artery. At least one of the arteries running to the legs must be flowing normally in order to perform this operation.

For inflow operations it is better to use artificial grafts. They perform well when the arterial flow is high and have been shown over years to provide durable results. The commonest material used for inflow operations is Dacron.

In general, with any graft, it is better to make the grafts as short as possible and to avoid crossing joints, but quite frequently, grafts have to be long and cross joints to salvage the leg and foot.

The grafts are stitched to the arteries using fine polypropylene stitches (similar to nylon). Permanent stitches are used because the joins between the grafts and the native artery require lifelong support. This is especially important when using artificial grafts.

What are the complications of bypass surgery? Complications of any operation can be divided into local and general.

Local complications:

- **Graft failure** – The bypass graft may block and the blood supply to the leg and foot will be reduced to the levels that were present before the bypass surgery. In fact, on many occasions when a bypass graft blocks, especially in the early period (hours to weeks) after surgery, the blood supply can be worse than before the bypass surgery. In these circumstances amputation can be inevitable unless the graft can be salvaged, and the blood supply restored.

ENDNOTES

- **Wound infection** – Wound infections are not uncommon in vascular bypass in the lower leg. This is because the incisions are long, the operations are prolonged, and the tissues of the leg are often already damaged and frequently swollen. Superficial wound infections are usually treatable by a combination of dressings, antibiotics and sometimes drainage of infection.

- **Graft infection** – If the infection involves the graft, especially if the graft is PTFE or Dacron, the situation is very much more serious. It is frequently impossible to eradicate infection from artificial materials and they need to be removed. When this happens the blood flow down the bypass graft is also removed. Unless an alternative route for a bypass graft can be found, this situation will frequently end in amputation. Graft infection is fortunately uncommon, probably only affecting about 5% of prosthetic grafts.

  - ➢ One particular type of graft infection can be critical for any type of graft. In this infection the surgical join (anastomosis) between the artery and the graft is involved. If this has occurred there is a risk of serious bleeding from the join as the seal becomes weakened by the infection.

- **Leg swelling** – This is a very common event after lower limb bypass surgery. It is due to a combination of factors. Much of it may resolve, but frequently persistent swelling is the price a patient pays to avoid amputation.

General complications:

- **Chest infections, heart attacks and strokes** – Because bypass surgery is prolonged and frequently takes place in elderly patients with other significant problems, these complications are not uncommon. However, they are just as common, if not more so, in patients undergoing amputation which is frequently the only alternative.

Will I need further treatment after my operation? All patients with hardening of the arteries should take a small dose of aspirin every day. As little as 75 milligrams of aspirin per day is beneficial and should be continued after your operation. Aspirin interferes with the function of platelets in the blood. Platelets are important in blood clotting and aspirin "thins" the blood making clots less likely to form. A new medication – clopidogrel (Plavix) – is being used more frequently. It has little

253

advantage over aspirin alone but there is increasing evidence that the combination of aspirin and clopidogrel may be more beneficial than either alone.

In some patients, aspirin alone is not considered a strong enough treatment to prevent blood clotting. In these patients, warfarin (Coumadin) can be used either alone or with aspirin to reduce the chances of clots. If you are taking warfarin tablets it is important that you have regular blood coagulation tests. These monitor how well the warfarin is working and ensure that it is kept under control.

What are the results of bypass surgery? The results of bypass surgery vary enormously depending on the type of graft (artificial or vein graft) inserted, the severity of the arterial disease and the site of the graft.

The larger grafts taking blood to the femoral arteries at the groin have good patency rates of 70-90% functioning normally at 5 years after surgery.

Femoro-femoral bypass grafts are durable with patency rates at 5 years between 74-90%. Early complications occurred in approximately one fifth of these patients within the first 30 days after surgery.

What is surveillance after lower extremity arterial bypass? The elements of a surveillance program after lower limb bypass grafting to enhance graft patency continue to evolve. Graft evaluation should include clinical assessment for new or changes in limb ischemia symptoms, measurement of ankle or toe systolic pressure, or both, and duplex ultrasound imaging of the bypass graft, which in the early postoperative period is predictive of the subsequent need for bypass graft revision. The natural history of moderate graft stenosis is known, and these lesions can be safely monitored using serial testing to identify progression. The testing frequency should be individualized to the patient, type of arterial bypass, and duplex scan findings. Graft surveillance should focus on the identification and repair of critical stenosis (peak systolic velocity exceeding 300 cm/s, and peak systolic velocity ratio across the stenosis exceeding 3.5) correlating with more than 70% diameter-reducing stenosis. A graft surveillance program should result in a graft failure rate of less than 3% per year.

[27] www.vascular.co.nz –http://www.vascular.co.nz/Bypass_surgery.htm

Chapter 28 — The Culprit

Risks Associated with Stenting — Complications associated with ureteral stenting include bleeding (usually minor and easily treated, but occasionally requiring transfusion); catheter migration or dislodgement (may require readjustment); coiling of the stent within the ureter (may cause lower abdominal pain or flank pain on urination, urinary frequency, or blood in the urine); introduction or worsening of infection; penetration of adjacent organs (e.g., bowel, gallbladder, or lungs).

Serious complications occur in approximately 4% of patients undergoing ureteral stenting, with minor complications in another 10%.

On another note, post-operative surgical infections kill a large number of people each year. These infections can be caused by something as minor as the bacteria on the patient's skin. They can be transmitted by medical attendants and instruments or even be airborne. These infections can be quite dangerous and are usually treated by large doses of antibiotics. This can lengthen the hospital stay and add thousands of dollars to a patient's hospital costs.

[28] Encyclopedia of Surgery – http://www.surgeryencycolpedia.com/ St-Wr/Ureteral-Stenting.html

Chapter 29 — Follow Up

Silent Killer — Endometriosis, medically speaking, is a benign form of cancer which attacks the uterus and female reproductive organs. When diagnosed with endometriosis, many patients are told the condition is painful, but not life threatening. What if that was all a lie?

While endometriosis, when isolated in reproductive organs, is not life threatening, what happens when this silent killer moves outside of its 'normal' realm? Endometriosis is not always a confined illness. When endometriosis moves out of the uterus and onto other organs, things can turn deadly.

After such diagnosis, one woman was told this form of endometriosis could pop up anywhere in the body. The heart, lungs, and brain were all fair game for her form of endometriosis. Small pieces of endometrial tissue could travel through the blood stream and set up house wherever it wanted... Unfortunately, endometriosis doesn't show up on CAT scans.

[29] AC Associated Content Lifestyle – http://www.associatedcontent. Com/article/396276/endometriosis_can_kill_a_doctors_lie_pg1.html

Silent Killer — There is a case in point, where this same woman reported after returning to surgery, her doctor found a large lump of scar tissue that the doctor was sure was nothing. He actually thought he was just doing her a favor in case the scarring was causing some of the pain she had been reporting. The test results proved this was no normal scar tissue. The lump was a large endometrial mass with its own blood supply. This living form of endometriosis was totally self sufficient and producing its own estrogen to enhance growth. The mass showed evidence of internal hemorrhage more than one time. The CAT scans she had been receiving were wrong and this endometrial cyst could have taken her life.

Endometriosis is a deadly benign cancer. Women should know the facts about endometriosis, regardless of what the doctors tell you. Endometriosis and endometrial cells can and will move through the blood stream and infect various parts of the body. The endometrial cells can embed in muscle tissue, heart tissue, lung tissue and brain tissue. Endometriosis is a deadly condition and under the right circumstances it can kill!

[30] AC Associated Content Lifestyle – http://www.associatedcontent. Com/article/396276/endometriosis_can_kill_a_doctors_lie_pg2.html

Silent Killer — In another case, a woman had her ovaries removed and her endometriosis came back – so she thought.

According to one medical expert, it is more likely that she had endometriosis still, as opposed to coming back. That is, it didn't "come back" because it was never really gone. In her case, the hormone replacement therapy that she was taking after her hysterectomy, stimulated the remaining implants and started causing her problems.

The risks that come when your ovaries stop producing estrogen, either naturally at menopause, or surgically induced, are increased incidence of heart disease, and also osteoporosis. Hence, hormone replacement therapy is still considered less of a risk as compared to heart disease and osteoporosis which both can kill you.

Her situation is a perfect example of why it is so important to remove all the endometriosis, no matter where it is. When endometriosis is left behind, by accident

256

or on purpose, the pain and problems can continue. Many women have been told that it is impossible to have endometriosis after their reproductive organs have been removed, but this is not the case. We stop having endometriosis when the endometriosis is removed.

Is hormone replacement therapy (HRT) necessary after hysterectomy or menopause? When a woman loses the estrogen that her ovaries produce, either through the natural aging process of menopause or more abruptly, through surgery, we need to think about the pros and cons of HRT. Estrogen helps protect a woman's bones against osteoporosis, it helps protect her heart from disease, and it has also been implicated as a help against Alzheimer's.

But HRT isn't always the right choice. Some cancers respond to estrogen, so women who have had these cancers or a close family member who has had them must weigh HRT very carefully.

Women with endometriosis were told for decades that HRT would bring back their endometriosis, and that they must do without it for months and months after surgery. The fact is, if all the endometriosis is completely removed at the time of the surgery, a woman has nothing to fear from HRT. Doctors routinely give the first replacement estrogen in the recovery room or a few days later.

On the other hand, if some endometriosis was left behind, by accident or by choice, then it doesn't seem to matter how long you wait to start HRT. The endometriosis that is still present may respond to the estrogen and begin to cause trouble. The key is that all the endometrioses must be completely removed. Then the decision about whether and when to begin HRT can be made on its own merits.

Can endometriosis be missed during surgery? When we see endometriosis after hysterectomy, it is generally in the exact same places it was in before the surgery. We think it's usually the same disease that was not removed, or not removed completely enough. It's more likely that you wouldn't have endometriosis *again*, but *still*.

It is further possible that endometriosis can be missed during surgery. Endometriosis can have many appearances, from very obvious to extremely subtle. If a surgeon is not thoroughly familiar with all the manifestations of endometriosis, it is possible that some will be missed.

Endometriosis can often hide underneath adhesions. When the surgeon removes the adhesions, the issue should be sent to the pathology lab for analysis. It is possible that endometriosis during surgery can be split or freed up as opposed to removed. The fact of having adhesions at all is suspicious, unless an obvious reason for an adhesion was found.

Also, endometriosis can hide. At surgery, every corner of the pelvis needs to be checked. After the ovaries are inspected, they need to be lifted up and held back, so the camera can go underneath them if not removed. A manipulator should be placed in the uterus so it can be pulled out of the way so the camera can go behind it. The bowel should be moved and examined, and so on.

Finally, although there are still much the doctors do not know about endometriosis, they do know that a little bit can sometimes cause great pain. If endometriosis was demonstrated at a previous surgery, and you are still experiencing pain, it is likely that the endometriosis is behind your present symptoms.

Will a hysterectomy cure endometriosis? Unfortunately, a hysterectomy will not cure endometriosis because not all of the endometriosis tissue can be removed. Most often, the endometriosis has already spread to other areas like the cervix, intestines, and bladder and if so, a hysterectomy may cure the erratic bleeding, but not the endometriosis.

[31] All Experts – http://en.allexperts.com/q/Endometriosis-1008/ Endometriosis-complete-hysterectomy.htm

Silent Killer — *Do I need pap smears after a hysterectomy?* Women who undergo total hysterectomy in which the cervix is removed along with the uterus do not need to have Pap smears, unless their hysterectomy was done because of cervical cancer or its precursors. Women who opt to keep their cervix during hysterectomy still need to continue having Pap smears. It's important to ask your surgeon whether you will still need Pap smears following your hysterectomy.

Whether or not your cervix is removed during your hysterectomy, you still need to have annual or bi-annual examinations at your gynecologist's office. During a post hysterectomy gynecology exam your doctor will examine your pelvic area for signs of cancer, as well as infections. You'll also be examined for signs of breast lumps. Remember to ask your doctor how often you need to return for examinations after your hysterectomy.

Who should have a Pap smear? When in doubt, ask your doctor. Remember, your doctor is your best source of health information. After a hysterectomy, ask whether your cervix was retained or removed. Although your doctor may have clarified this prior to surgery, there are times when during surgery, the doctor decides to remove or keep the cervix. If you are unsure about whether your cervix has been removed or not, ask your doctor.

[32] About.com: Women's Health – http://womenshealth.about.com/od/hysterectomy/f/papafterhyst.htm

Chapter 30 — First Year

Estrogens and Menopause — Estrogen is the most important hormone that influences the life of women. Estrogen is a hormone responsible for female sexual features such as breast development and the menstrual cycle. For young women, puberty starts when the production of estrogen increases in the ovules. The estrogen level remains relatively the same during 25 years, after which it will decrease constantly. Since the number of ovules that mature in the ovary decrease as women get older, the formation of estrogen also decreases. The body tries to fight this problem by producing two other hormones by the hypophyse: the Ovule Stimulating Hormone (FSH) and the Luetinisante Hormone (LH).

However, the decreased levels of estrogen and increased production of FSH and LH create symptoms such as hot flashes or night sweat.

There are three principle forms of estrogen found in the human body estrone, estradiol and estriol. Estradiol is the most commonly measured type of estrogen for nonpregnant women. The amount of estradiol in the blood varies through her menstrual cycle. After menopause, estradiol production drops to a very low but constant level.

When estrogen levels decrease and menopause starts, the main risks become osteoporosis and arteriosclerosis. HRT was supposed to be the wonder drug that would improve the quality of life during menopause. However, as the active hormones have other important functions in the body; it is possible to have unwanted effects. Estradial (an estrogen) intervenes in various cancers. High level of estrogen will increase the risk for breast cancer. Conventional hormone therapy is not the only option available. Women who do not wish to take hormones may use isoflavones supplements.

³³ Insoflavones.info – http://www.isoflavones.info/estrogen.php

Chapter 33 — Reflections

Near Death Experiences — According to LiveScience in an article titled: *Near-Death Experiences: What Really Happens?* Many reports of near-death experiences sound the same: a welcoming white light and a replay of memories. But now scientists aim to study what really happens to the brain and consciousness when someone is on the verge of dying.

In a new study called AWARE (Awareness during Resuscitation), doctors will examine patients in hospitals in Europe and North America who reach a state called cardiac arrest. "Contrary to popular perception, death is not a specific moment," said leader of the study Dr. Sam Parnia of the University of Southampton in the U.K. "It is a process that begins when the heart stops beating, the lungs stop working and the brain ceases functioning – a medical condition termed cardiac arrest, which from a biological viewpoint is synonymous with clinical death."

Science has long struggled to define death, and to determine when the precise moment of death occurs. Now though, most doctors consider death more of a process than an event. A person is thought to have died when he/she stops breathing, his/her heart stops beating, and his/her brain activity ceases.

"During a cardiac arrest, all three criteria of death are present," Parnia said. "There then follows a period of time, which may last from a few seconds to an hour or more, in which emergency medical efforts may succeed in restarting the heart and reversing the dying process. What people experience during this period of cardiac arrest provides a unique window of understanding into what we are all likely to experience during the dying process."

Previous research suggests about 10 to 20 percent of people who live through cardiac arrest report lucid, well-structured thought processes, reasoning, memories and sometimes detailed recall of events during their encounter with death. One study found that people who reported peaceful feelings, bright light, and out-of-body experiences during a brush with death are more likely to have had difficulty separating sleep from wakefulness in their everyday lives. Both before and after their near-death experiences, these people often have symptoms of the rapid-eye movement (REM) state of sleep while awake.

The AWARE researchers want to find out what happens to the brain when a person's body has started to shut down, whether it is possible for people to see and hear during cardiac arrest, and what's going on during out of body experiences.

[34] Live Science – http://www.livescience.com/health/080912- near-death.html

Chapter 34 — Endometriosis

Endometriosis — Endometriosis is a painful, chronic disease that affects five and half million women and girls in the USA and Canada, and millions more worldwide. It occurs when tissue like that which lines the uterus (tissue called the endometrium) is found outside the uterus – usually in the abdomen on the ovaries, fallopian tubes, and ligaments that support the uterus; the area between the vagina and rectum; the outer surface of the uterus; and the lining of the pelvic cavity. Other sites for these endometrial growths may include the bladder, bowel, vagina, cervix, vulva, and in abdominal surgical scars. Less commonly they are found in the lung, arm, thigh, and other locations.

This misplaced tissue develops into growths or lesions which respond to the menstrual cycle in the same way that the tissue of the uterine lining does: each month the tissue builds up, breaks down, and sheds. Menstrual blood flows from the uterus and out of the body through the vagina, but the blood and tissue shed from endometrial growths has no way of leaving the body. This results in internal bleeding, breakdown of the blood and tissue from the lesions, and inflammation – and can cause pain, infertility, scar tissue formation, adhesions, and bowel problems.

[35] Endo-Online – http://www.endometriosisassn.org/endo.html

Endometriosis — The cause of endometriosis is unknown. The retrograde menstruation theory (transtubal migration theory) suggests that during menstruation some of the menstrual tissue backs up through the fallopian tubes, implants in the abdomen, and grows. Some experts believe that all women experience some menstrual tissue backup and that an immune system problem or a hormonal problem allows this tissue to grow in the women who develop endometriosis.

Another theory suggests that endometrial tissue is distributed from the uterus to other parts of the body through the lymph system or through the blood system. A genetic theory suggests that it may be carried in the genes in certain families or that some families may have predisposing factors to endometriosis.

Surgical transplantation has also been cited in many cases where endometriosis is found in abdominal scars, although it has also been found in such scars when accidental implantation seems unlikely.

Another theory suggests that remnants of tissue from when the woman was an embryo may later develop into endometriosis, or that some adult tissues retain the ability they had in the embryo stage to transform reproductive tissue in certain circumstances.

[36] Endo-Online – http://www.endometriosisassn.org/endo.html

Endometriosis — On another note, research by the Endometriosis Association revealed a startling link between dioxin (TCCD) exposure and the development of endometriosis. Dioxin is a toxic chemical byproduct of pesticide manufacturing, bleached pulp and paper products, and medical and municipal waste incineration. The EA discovered a colony of rhesus monkeys that had developed endometriosis after exposure to dioxin. 79% of the monkeys exposed to dioxin developed endometriosis, and, in addition, the more dioxin exposure, the more severe the endometriosis.

[37] Endo-Online – http://www.endometriosisassn.org/endo.html

Endometriosis FAQ — *What is endometriosis?* Endometriosis is a common health problem in women. It gets its name from the word, endometrium, the tissue that lines the uterus or womb. Endometriosis occurs when this tissue grows outside of the uterus on other organs or structures in the body.

Most often, endometriosis is found on the: ovaries, fallopian tubes, tissues that hold the uterus in place, outer surface of the uterus, and lining of the pelvic cavity. Other sites for growths can include the vagina, cervix, vulva, bowel, bladder, or rectum. In rare cases, endometriosis has been found in other parts of the body, such as the lungs, brain, and skin.

What are the symptoms of endometriosis? The most common symptom of endometriosis is pain in the lower abdomen or pelvis, or the lower back, mainly during menstrual periods. The amount of pain a woman feels does not depend on how much endometriosis she has. Some women have no pain, even though their disease affects large areas. Other women with endometriosis have severe pain even though they have only a few small growths.

Symptoms of endometriosis can include very painful menstrual cramps (pain may get worse over time), chronic pain in the lower back and pelvis, pain during or after sex, intestinal pain, painful bowel movements or painful urination during menstrual periods, spotting or bleeding between menstrual periods, infertility or not being able to get pregnant, fatigue, and diarrhea, constipation, bloating, or nausea, especially during menstrual periods.

Recent research shows a link between other health problems in women with endometriosis and their families. Some of these include: allergies, asthma, and chemical sensitivities; autoimmune diseases, in which the body's system that fights illness attacks itself instead – these can include hypothyroidism, multiple sclerosis, and lupus; chronic fatigue syndrome (CFS) and fibromyalgia; being more likely to get infections and mononucleosis; mitral valve prolapsed, a condition in which one of the heart's valves does not close as tightly as normal; frequent yeast infections; and certain cancers, such as ovarian, breast, endocrine, kidney, thyroid, brain, and colon cancers, and melanoma and non-Hodgkin's lymphoma.

Why does endometriosis cause pain and health problems? Growths of endometriosis are benign (not cancerous). But they still can cause many problems. To see why, it helps to understand a woman's menstrual cycle. Every month, hormones cause the lining of a woman's uterus to build up with tissue and blood vessels. If a woman does not get pregnant, the uterus sheds this tissue and blood. It comes out of the body through the vagina as her menstrual period.

Patches of endometriosis also respond to the hormones produced during the menstrual cycle. With the passage of time, the growths of endometriosis may expand by adding extra tissue and blood. The symptoms of endometriosis often get worse.

Tissue and blood that is shed into the body can cause inflammation, scar tissue, and pain. As endometrial tissue grows, it can cover or grow into the ovaries and block the fallopian tubes. Trapped blood in the ovaries can form cysts, or closed sacs. It also can cause inflammation and cause the body to form scar tissue and adhesions, tissue that sometimes binds organs together. This scar tissue may cause pelvic pain and make it hard for women to get pregnant. The growths can also cause problems in the intestines and bladder.

Who gets endometriosis? More than five million women in the United States have endometriosis. It is one of the most common health problems for women. It can occur in any teen or woman who has menstrual periods, but it is most common in women in their 30s and 40s.

The symptoms of endometriosis stop for a time during pregnancy. Symptoms also tend to decrease with menopause, when menstrual periods end for good. In some cases, women who take menopausal hormone therapy may still have symptoms of endometriosis.

What can raise my chances of getting endometriosis? You might be more likely to get endometriosis if you have: never had children, menstrual periods that last more than seven days, short menstrual cycles (27 days or less), a family member (mother, aunt, sister) with endometriosis, a health problem that prevents normal passage of menstrual blood flow, and damage to cells in the pelvis from an infection.

How can I reduce my chances of getting endometriosis? There are no definite ways to lower your chances of getting endometriosis. Yet, since the hormone estrogen is involved in thickening the lining of the uterus during the menstrual cycle, you can try to lower levels of estrogen in your body.

To keep lower estrogen levels in your body, you can: exercise regularly, keep a low amount of body fat, and avoid large amounts of alcohol and drinks with caffeine.

Why is it important to find out if I have endometriosis? The pain of endometriosis can interfere with your life. Studies show that women with endometriosis often skip school, work, and social events. This health problem can also get in the way of relationships with your partner, friends, children, and co-workers. Plus, endometriosis can make it hard for you to get pregnant.

Finding out that you have endometriosis is the first step in taking back your life. Many treatments can control the symptoms. Medicine can relieve your pain. When endometriosis causes fertility problems, surgery can boost your chances of getting pregnant.

How do I know that I have endometriosis? If you have symptoms of this disease, talk with your doctor or your obstetrician/ gynecologist (OB/GYN). An OB/GYN has special training to diagnose and treat this condition. Sometimes endometriosis is mistaken for other health problems that cause pelvic pain and the exact cause might be hard to pinpoint.

The doctor will talk to you about your symptoms and health history. The doctor may also do these tests to check for clues of endometriosis:

- **Pelvic exam.** Your doctor will perform a pelvic exam to feel for large cysts or scars behind your uterus. Smaller areas of endometriosis are hard to feel.

- **Ultrasound.** Your doctor could perform an ultrasound, an imaging test to see if there are ovarian cysts from endometriosis. During a vaginal ultrasound, the doctor will insert a wand-shaped scanner into your vagina. During an ultrasound of your pelvis, a scanner is moved across your abdomen. Both tests use sound waves to make pictures of your reproductive organs. Magnetic resonance imaging (MRI) is another common imaging test that can produce a picture of the inside of your body.

- **Laparoscopy.** The only way for your doctor to know for sure that you have endometriosis is to look inside your abdomen to see endometriosis tissue. He or she can do this through a minor surgery called laparoscopy. You will receive general anesthesia before the surgery. Then, your abdomen is expanded with gas to make it easy to see your organs. A tiny cut is made in your abdomen and a thin tube with a light is placed inside to see growths from endometriosis. Sometimes doctors can diagnose endometriosis just by seeing the growths. Other times, they need to take a small sample of tissue and study it under a microscope.

If your doctor does not find signs of an ovarian cyst during an ultrasound, before doing a laparoscopy, your doctor may prescribe birth control pills to control your menstrual cycle. Sometimes this treatment helps lessen pelvic pain during your period. Some doctors may offer another treatment that blocks the menstrual cycle and lowers the amount of estrogen your body makes before doing a laparoscopy. This treatment is a medicine called a gonadotropin releasing hormone (GnRH) agonist, which also may help pelvic pain. If your pain improves on this medicine, the doctor will likely think that you have endometriosis.

Laparoscopy is often recommended for diagnosis and treatment if the pelvic pain persists, even after taking birth control pills and pain medicine.

What causes endometriosis? No one knows for sure what causes this disease, but experts have a number of theories:

- Since endometriosis runs in families, it may be carried in the genes, or some families have traits that make them more likely to get it.

- Endometrial tissue may move from the uterus to other body parts through the blood system or lymph system.

- If a woman has a faulty immune system, it will fail to find and destroy endometrial tissue growing outside of the uterus. Recent research shows that immune system disorders and certain cancers are more common in women with endometriosis.

- The hormone estrogen appears to promote the growth of endometriosis. So, some research is looking at whether it is a disease of the endocrine system, the body's system of glands, hormones, and other secretions.

- Endometrial tissue has been found in abdominal scars and might have been moved there by mistake during a surgery.

- Small amounts of tissue from when a woman was an embryo might later become endometriosis.

- New research shows a link between dioxin exposure and getting endometriosis. Dioxin is a toxic chemical from the making of pesticides and the burning of wastes. More research is needed to find out whether man-made chemicals cause endometriosis.

- Endometrial tissue may back up into the abdomen through the fallopian tubes during a woman's monthly period. This transplanted tissue could grow outside of the uterus. However, most experts agree that this theory does not entirely explain why endometriosis develops.

How is endometriosis treated? There is no cure for endometriosis, but there are many treatments for the pain and infertility that it causes. Talk with your doctor about what option is best for you. The treatment you choose will depend on your symptoms, age, and plans for getting pregnant.

- **Pain Medication.** For some women with mild symptoms, doctors may suggest taking over-the-counter medicines for pain. These include ibuprofen (Advil and Motrin) or naproxen (Aleve). When these medicines don't help, doctors may prescribe stronger pain relievers.
- **Hormone Treatment.** When pain medicine is not enough, doctors often recommend hormone medicines to treat endometriosis. Only women who do not wish to become pregnant can use these drugs. Hormone treatment is best for women with small growths who do not have bad pain. Hormones come in many forms including pills, shots, and nasal sprays. Common hormones used for endometriosis include:
  - ➤ **Birth control pills** to decrease the amount of menstrual flow and prevent overgrowth of tissue that lines the uterus. Most birth control pills contain two hormones, estrogen, and progestin. Once a woman stops taking them, she can get pregnant again. Stopping these pills will cause the symptoms of endometriosis to return.
  - ➤ **GnRH agonists and antagonists** greatly reduce the amount of estrogen in a woman's body, which stops the menstrual cycle. These drugs should not be used alone because they can cause side effects similar to those during menopause, such as hot flashes, bone loss, and vaginal dryness. Taking a low dose of progestin or estrogen along with these drugs can protect against these side effects. When a woman stops taking this medicine, monthly periods, and the ability to get pregnant return. She also might stay free of the problems of endometriosis for months or years afterward.
  - ➤ **Progestin.** The hormone progestin can shrink spots of endometriosis by working against the effects of estrogen on the tissue. It will stop a woman's menstrual periods but can cause irregular vaginal bleeding. Medroxprogesterone is a common progestin taken as a shot. Side effects of progestin can include weight gain, depressed mood, and decreased bone growth.
  - ➤ **Danazol** is a weak male hormone that lowers the levels of estrogen and progesterone in a woman's body. This stops a

267

woman's period or makes it come less often. It is not often the first choice for treatment due to its side effects, such as oily skin, weight gain, tiredness, smaller breasts, and facial hair growth. It does not prevent pregnancy and can harm a baby growing in the uterus. It also cannot be used with other hormones, such as birth control pills.

- **Surgery.** Surgery is usually the best choice for women with severe endometriosis – many growths, a great deal of pain, or fertility problems. There are both minor and more complex surgeries that can help. Your doctor might suggest one of the following:
    - ➢ **Laparoscopy** can be used to diagnose and treat endometriosis. During this surgery, doctors remove growths and scar tissue or burn them away. The goal is to treat the endometriosis without harming the healthy tissue around it. Women recover from laparoscopy much faster than from major abdominal surgery.
    - ➢ **Laparotomy or major abdominal surgery** that involves a much larger cut in the abdomen than with laparoscopy. This allows the doctor to reach and remove growths of endometriosis in the pelvic or abdomen.
    - ➢ **Hysterectomy** is a surgery in which the doctor removes the uterus. Removing the ovaries as well can help ensure that endometriosis will not return. This is done when the endometriosis has severely damaged these organs. A woman cannot get pregnant after this surgery, so it should only be considered as a last resort.

How do I cope with a disease that has no cure? You may feel many emotions – sadness, fright, anger, confusion, and loneliness. It is important to get support to cope with endometriosis. Consider joining a support group to talk with other women who have endometriosis. There are support groups on the Internet and in many communities.

It is also important to learn as much as you can about the disease. Talking with friends, family, and your doctor can help.

ENDNOTES

Where can I get more information about this disease? You can find out more about endometriosis by contacting womenshealth.gov at 1-800-994-9662. You also can contact the following organizations:

Endometriosis Association
Phone Number: (414) 355-2200
Internet Address: http://www.endometriosisassn.org
The American College of Obstetricians
and Gynecologists
Phone Numbers: (202) 638-5577; (202) 863-2518
(for publication requests only)
Internet Address: http://www.acog.org

Endometriosis Research Center
Phone Number: (561) 274-7442
Internet Address: http://www.endocenter.org
Eunice Kennedy Shriver National Institute of Child
Health and Human Development
Phone Number: 1-800-370-2943
TTY: 1-888-320-6942
Internet Address: http://www.nichd.nih.gov

This FAQ was reviewed by:
Esther Eisenberg, M.D., M.P.H.
Professor of Obstetrics and Gynecology
Vanderbilt University Medical Center
Medical Officer
Reproductive Science Branch
Eunice Kennedy Shriver National Institute of Child
Health and Human Development
National Institutes of Health
Content last updated November 1, 2009.
[38] Womenshealth.gov – http://www.womenshealth.gov/faq/endometriosis.cfm

Author Photo © 2023 Edwin Wolfe

LORI ANN MOESZINGER also known as simply "L" is the face behind The Ridge Publishing Group and its imprints. She is an American author, blogger, and publisher who resides in Coeur d'Alene, Idaho, with her husband and two dogs. She writes under the pseudonyms: Ann Patterson for her business law pieces; L. A. Moeszinger for her writing, publishing, and marketing pieces; Lori Ann Moeszinger for her biblical books and personal pieces; and a handful of others for her series, The Manhattan Diaries. She believes strongly in faith, blessings, and working her butt off . . . and she thinks one of the best things about being an author-publisher—unlike the lawyer she used to be—is that she can let her passion out.

Transcending her former life as a lawyer, Lori now revels in the freedom of expression that authorship and publishing afford—a stark contrast to the rigid confines of law. Her new chapter is one marked by a fervent passion for empowering others, a commitment to hard work, and the joy of sharing her literary gifts.

Discover the multifaced worlds Lori has woven at her websites and blog sites, or connect with her on her social media platforms where she continues to inspire, educate, and transform the written word into a shared experience of growth and discovery.

Parent Website: https://www.RidgePublishingGroup.com and

    blog site https://www.PublisherAndHerWorld.com

Publisher Website: https://www.GuardiansofBiblicalTruth.com and

    blog site https://www.Jesus-Says.com

Author website: https://www.LAMoeszinger.com and New Youniversity sites:

    https://www.NewYouniversity.com, https://www.ManhattanChronicles.com

Bridge Website: https://www.AuthorsDoor.com and

    blog site https://www.AuthorsRedDoor.com

Entertainment website: https://www.EthanFoxBooks.com and

    blog site https://www.KidsStagram.com

Want More?

Welcome to Coffee with God! Jesus-Says! Dive into our blog for inspiring insights and biblical truths that deepen your faith and enrich your spiritual journey. Explore thought-provoking articles, personal testimonies, and practical guidance rooted in Scripture. Whether you're new to the faith or a lifelong believer, Jesus-Says.com offers wisdom and encouragement for your walk with Christ. Join our community and grow in your relationship with God!

Guardians of Biblical Truth Hub

Welcome to our Guardians of Biblical Truth Facebook page! Join our community to deepen your understanding of the Bible and live out its principles. Engage in enriching Bible studies, share faith testimonies, and connect with like-minded believers. Whether you're new to the faith or a seasoned believer, you'll find support and inspiration here. Join us and grow in your walk with Christ.

Guardians of Biblical Truth Forum

Welcome to our Guardians of Biblical Truth Forum! Join our closed Facebook group to deepen your understanding of the Bible and strengthen your faith. Engage in enriching discussions, share personal testimonies, and connect with a supportive community of believers. Whether you're new to the faith or a seasoned believer, you'll find inspiration and encouragement here. Join us today and grow in your walk with Christ!